THE GAME OF DESTINY -
Fortune Telling with Lenormand Cards
by Mario dos Ventos
1st Edition, January 2007
All rights reserved
Printed: 208 pages, 8.5' x 11.0', with illustrations of the *1941 Mlle Lenormand Cartomancy Deck* published and copyrighted by Piatnik, Austria
Publisher: Nzo Quimbanda Exu Ventania
ISBN: 978-1-84753-109-4
Printed: Lulu Publishing
License: Standard Copyright License
Copyright Year: © January 2007, Mario dos Ventos

All rights reserved.
No parts of this book may be reproduced or transmitted in any form or by any reasons, electrical, or mechanical, including photocopying, recording, or information storage and retrieval system without written permission from the author, except for the inclusion of brief quotations in a review. Breach of copyright will be persecuted!

THE GAME OF DESTINY -
Fortune Telling with Lenormand Cards

by

Mario dos Ventos

Nzo Quimbanda Exu Ventania
www.exu.moonfruit.com
under the watchful eyes of the Maioral

CONTENTS

Dedication	Page 9
Introduction	Page 11

Part I
The Cards

Card 1 – The Cavalier	Page 19
Card 2 – The Clover	Page 22
Card 3 – The Ship	Page 25
Card 4 – The House	Page 28
Card 5 – The Tree	Page 31
Card 6 – The Clouds	Page 34
Card 7 – The Snake	Page 37
Card 8 – The Coffin	Page 40
Card 9 – The Flowers	Page 43
Card 10 – The Scythe	Page 45
Card 11 – The Whip	Page 49
Card 12 – The Birds	Page 52
Card 13 – The Child	Page 55
Card 14 – The Fox	Page 58
Card 15 – The Bear	Page 61
Card 16 – The Star	Page 64
Card 17 – The Stork	Page 67
Card 18 – The Dog	Page 70
Card 19 – The Tower	Page 73
Card 20 – The Garden	Page 76
Card 21 – The Mountain	Page 79
Card 22 – The Ways	Page 82
Card 23 – The Mouse	Page 85
Card 24 – The Heart	Page 88
Card 25 – The Ring	Page 91
Card 26 – The Book	Page 94

Card 27 – The Letter	Page 97
Card 28 – The Gentleman	Page 100
Card 29 – The Lady	Page 103
Card 30 – The Lily	Page 106
Card 31 – The Sun	Page 109
Card 32 – The Moon	Page 112
Card 33 – The Key	Page 115
Card 34 – The Fishes	Page 118
Card 35 – The Anchor	Page 121
Card 36 – The Cross	Page 124
Additional Combinations and Special Meanings	
- Cards indicating Persons	Page 127
- Cards indicating Times and Time Frames	Page 128
- Concerning Relationships	Page 129
- Concerning Work and Employment	Page 130
- Concerning Friendships	Page 131
- Concerning Financial Matters	Page 131
- Concerning Health	Page 133
- Concerning Domestic Life	Page 136
- Mystical & Spiritual Meanings of the Cards	Page 137

Part II
Spreads   Page 143

Part III
Other Aspects of the Work

Divination with the Help of a Gypsy Spirit	Page 153
Blessing the Deck	Page 156
Macumba - Cleaning up the Client's Destiny	Page 158
Personal Notes	Page 176
Sample Spreads	Page 178

Appendix
Lenormand through the years   Page 191

Bibliography   Page 197

About the Author   Page 199

Other Books by the Same Author   Page 201

Further Study   Page 207

DEDICATION

To Cigana Maria Madalenna

My beautiful 'Gypsy of Faith',
who opened my eyes to the mysteries of these cards.

Sarava Cigana!

INTRODUCTION

Marie-Anne Adélaïde Lenormand
27 May 1772 – 25 June 1843

Marie-Anne Adélaïde Lenormand was beyond any doubt one of the most famous and most talented fortune tellers of all times. Her life is also surrounded with stories of amazement and mystery. She was born into a merchant's family on the 27th of May 1772 in Saint-Léonard, a part of the town of Alençon in Normandy, Northern France. An active child who didn't like to be confined to the house, Marie-Anne loved the outdoors and many days left her mother's home early in the morning to return only after sunset. She loved the company of Artists and had a strong affection with the Gypsy people, who were in those days not allowed inside the city. It was a Gypsy who read her palm and told her that she would one day find fame and fortune far away from home. Typically for the time in which she lived, Marie-Anne started her working life at the age of eleven. She bought her first set of cards from the Gypsies with the money she made as a seamstress and laundry woman. It was also the Gypsy people who taught her how to read the cards and tell the future.

Her family moved to Paris in 1786 after Marie-Anne's mother remarried - her father died when she was only one year old! Her stepfather owned a successful lingerie business and Marie-Anne began to use her special gift of Cartomancy to read for her stepfather's wealthy and somewhat infamous female clients - those, who made their living in what is sometimes called 'the oldest business on earth'. Her precise predictions helped spread her fame fast and her clientele grew quickly. Only 19 years old, Marie-Anne opened her own bookstore in Faubourg Saint-Germain, Rue de Tournon No 5, in the year 1793. This store however was only used as a cover for her card reading business, as fortune telling by cards and astrology were still illegal practices in France at that time. With the money she made from fortune telling, Marie-Anne bought a country house in Migneaux in 1802 and a flat in Paris, on Rue de la Sante, in the same year. She also owned a Chateau near Poissy and another country estate near Alencon. But with fame and wealth also came envy, and Marie-Anne was more then once brought before the judge to defend herself against accusations of fortune telling and astrology - professions considered illegal in France in the 19th century. She was accused of making 20.000 Francs per year by calculating horoscopes and employing other means of divination.

This was an enormous amount of money in relation to the average income of France at that time. Records show that she was persecuted and even served a sentence at *Madelonettes*, one of the prisons of Paris. The last time she was arrested by the Parisian police was on December 15th 1809, but among her clients were enough influential members of the judicial system as well as politicians to prevent her from further harm. Robespierre, Mirabeau, Camille Desmoulins, Danton, as well as countless foreign ambassadors and even the King of Naples - all these celebrities of her era consulted her. Some sources even mention her involvement in the weather forecast with numerous Parisian newspapers.

Josephine de Beauharnais and her husband Napoleon Bonaparte sought out her counsel also. It is said that Mlle Lenormand foretold the French Revolution, Napoleon and Josephine's divorce and the rise and fall of Napoleon. Marie-Anne first met Napoleon when he was a general in the French army. She predicted that he would go to war with Italy and that all of France would know his name when he returned triumphantly. Bonaparte also visited her in 1812 to inquire about his planed invasion of Russia. She counseled him against his ventures and told him that it would only end in a disaster - which it did. She also predicted the death of Joachim Marat, Napolean's cavalry leader. It is said that in consultation with Mlle. Lenormand, Marat repeatedly drew the King of Diamonds until she finally threw the cards at him and declared he was to die at the gallows or be executed by a firing squad. Marat was indeed executed by firing squad in 1815.

Marie-Anne did most of her consultations in her flat in Paris, and her involvement with artists and actors made her 'perform in style' - sitting in front of a colorful wall carpet, turban on her head and many gold rings on her fingers. Due to her popularity, queues formed in front of her house, which sometimes had to be broken off by the French police. She began writing her memoirs in 1814 - aged 42 - and revealed much delicate information about many of the 'great men of France' who sought her counsel. Her 1820 published work *Mémoires historiques et secrets de l'impératrice Joséphine* in which she wrote about her encounters with Napoleon Bonaparte and Queen Josephine created a huge scandal in France, and were translated into German and English due to their best-selling nature. Following this scandal and the bad press it created for her, Marie-Anne moved to Belgium in February 1821. She set up her fortune telling business in Brussels and clients from all over Europe started flooding in soon after. But luck was not on her side entirely. She was arrested by the Belgian police in April of the same year, and sentenced to a monetary fine. Convicted of the illegal practice of fortune telling, she also had to serve a prison sentence of one year. But she appealed against the court's decision and was set free in August of the same year. Marie-Anne returned to Paris and published *Souvenir de la Belgique*, a book about her adventures in Belgium. It is said that she traveled to London, England in 1792 and then again in 1822 to join a secret society called *Members of the Mercurii*.

Marie-Anne never married and had no children - she was in fact very masculine in appearance and many whispers say that she preferred the company of women to that of men. Mlle Lenormand predicted for herself a life span of 124 years, but she died alone on June 25th 1843 in Paris, aged 71. Her own predictions told her to stay away from hospitals and physicians, and she indeed died following an operation on her bladder. Her funeral was attended by hundreds of her clients, the church overflowing with candles and flowers. She lays buried in Paris' *Pere Lachaise Cemetery* and her grave is to this day well tended.

The Game of Destiny

Two years after Marie-Anne Lenormand's death, the publishing house Grimaud makes the first mention of a set of fortune telling cards called *Grand jeu de Mademoiselle Lenormand* - The Great Cards of Mlle Lenormand. This deck was created by a woman called Madame Breteau, who claimed to have been a student of Marie-Anne. Made up of 54 cards, the deck contained astrological symbols and depictions of Greek and Roman myths and legends. It is still available today. The cards this book deals with were published in 1850 by Dorndorf, a publishing house in Germany, and are today widely known as *Petit Lenormand* - the Small Lenormand deck. Other names for these cards are *The French Cartomancy Deck* and, in Brazil, *O Barhalo Cigano*, The Gypsy Deck.

Marie-Anne Lenormand obviously never used these cards. What we know is that she employed Tarot and playing cards, Palmistry, Astrology, tea leaves and a specially prepared mirror in her work. It is no secret that she was exceptionally psychically gifted and that she used her own intuition as well as the information obtained from her Gypsy friends in her predictions – not to forget her spirit guide Ariel! The meanings and interpretations given in this book were collected from published and verbal sources, obtained from readers and fortune tellers who used this deck for many decades.

Mlle Lenormand also used the *Petit Etteillas* deck in most of her readings but never gave any instructions on to how to employ these cards in any of her many books. Even though Jean-Baptiste Alliette, the father of the *Petit Etteillas*, published a thorough book containing instructions on how to divine with his cards, we know that Mlle Lenormand used a more simple way of reading.

The interpretations for single cards as well as card combination given in this book are presented in a plain and neutral fashion wherever possible. This is to transfer a basic meaning to the reader, who will have to use his or her intuition in using the cards. Not to forget that, depending on its position in the game and especially in relation to the Person Card, a meaning can either indicate the future ('*you are going to…*') or the past ('*you have/had….*'). All in all, we have over 1260 possible combinations of either 2 or more cards. How to determine which cards speak about the future and which reveal past happenings will be explained more closely in the section on Card Spreads.

Symbolically speaking, each of the 36 cards represents a colorful strand of information. The skilled reader or fortune teller will be able to create a meaningful and clear tapestry, allowing the colors and meanings of individual strands/cards to surface when ever appropriate, to be interwoven in a way that can help the client to understand his or her destiny better. Divination after all is more then simple 'fortune telling'. It is the art of accessing divine information related to the client's destiny and life-path. Every reader or diviner needs to remember, that it is their duty to help their clients to align themselves with their destiny and to achieve a life of health, wealth, happiness and fulfillment. If this alignment can not be provided during the ritual of divination, then it is nothing more then a game and useless past-time.

Reading for clients

In general we can say that cards pointing towards the past are 'in the back of the **Person Card** (see page 127 under 'Additional Combinations and Special Meanings') and cards speaking about the future are 'in front' of the person card. Back and front can be understood as the directions into which the card 'looks'. In this deck, the *Nr 1941 Mlle Lenormand Cartomancy Deck*, a version of the *Petit Lenormand* produced by the Austrian card manufacturer PIATNIK, it is safe to say that **The Lady** looks towards the left, **The Gentleman** looks towards the right. Other, more modern decks have changed the direction into which these two cards 'look' and are not recommended to be used in conjunction with this book. It is best to stick with the *1941 Mlle Lenormand Cartomancy Deck* published by PIATNIK or the so called *Blue Owl Lenormand cards* - named after the image of a blue owl on the back of the card - and even the *Mystical Lenormand*, both published by the Swiss company AG Müller Urania. The *French Cartomancy Deck* and the Lenorman deck published by Llewellyn Publications in the US, even though beautiful in appearance, can unfortunately not be used with this book.

Also included in this present book are card interpretations related to occupations, natural habitats and a small section on interpretations related to Umbanda and Quimbanda, which can easily be ignored by those who are not affiliated or inclined to work with either of these traditions. For reasons of simplicity, this section is called Macumba. Not a valid tradition in itself, this term is often used in Brazil (particularly in Rio de Janeiro) to describe African based spiritual and religious traditions.

Divination, fortune telling and spiritual work are rewarding professions - not just monetary, but also emotionally. People will hopefully notice any gift you have. With the quality of your readings your clientele should increase. It speaks for the quality of your predictions if your clients return and if your fame spreads by word of mouth. What you want to be wary of however is for people to develop an addiction to your talent

If you decide to also offer other services besides card reading, and in turn starting to charge people, then keep in mind that your clients were not set on this planet to make you rich. Many readers will not see the same clients more then 2 - 4 times per year, either every 6 or every 3 months. Tell your clients from the start that you are not able to help them with every single problem, but that there are certain areas in their life where they have to make their own decisions. It is from those decisions and the experiences which follow that we learn and progress in life. In my personal practice I had people calling me or emailing me 5 or 6 times per day. People have threatened me that they would destroy my reputation and find other workers and readers who would take on their case if I would not do as they wish! This situation is not unique to me, but many other readers have reported similar happenings. Don't let your clients bully or threaten you! If people want to find someone else, then let them - it is better to have fewer clients who appreciate your work and help you keep your sanity, then a hand full of lunatics who need your attention 24 hours each day and will only drain you.

Always take payment before you start your reading. It is very common for readers of Afro-Cuban and Afro-Brazilian traditions, such as Santeria, Candomble, Umbanda and Quimbanda, to fold notes and to make the sign of the cross at the beginning of each consultation. Alternatively, readers have the clients fold the money and make the sign of the cross on him or herself, before handing it to the reader. An exchange of money is also an exchange of energy. To actively involve the money you charge for your readings can also enrich the quality of the information you pass on to your client - and no, this is not related to Psychometry, the 'art' of picking up information from objects.

Tell people what you see, not what they want to hear! It can be very tempting to tell a sick client that his or her health is 'just fine' and that all ailments will be sorted out shortly. But remember that this is not always the case. I have personally sent many clients to see a physician when they came to me to only ask about their finances and matters of love. But this honesty has always paid off, especially when previously undetected health issues have been identified through divination and further harm to the client's health have been prevented. How many times would I have loved to tell a woman that the man they are involved with will leave his wife to live with them - but it hardly ever happens that the dreams of those clients actually come true exactly as they hope and wish! With all this in mind, never forget to use your common sense and use the information revealed in the cards carefully. If you see that the client's health is in danger, tell them to go for a check up or stick with their medication. If you see that their partner is cheating on them, then try and tell them to spend more time in their relationship. All in all, use the information you obtain from the cards wisely and do not abuse your clients trust!

Offer your clients aftercare. It is all good to read the future and to advise your clients of the right choices to take, but this is sometimes not enough. Sometimes luck needs a little push, and this is where Part III of this book comes into play. If you feel that offering spiritual work in addition to your reading would benefit your clients, then you can use the information at the end of this book to help your clients with matters of love, luck and success. If you feel that this is not for you, then simply leave it out or try and refer clients to someone who might be able to offer these services. Whatever you want to do, always measure how far you want to go, what level of risk you want to take according to your spiritual path and how deeply you want to get involved with your clients. Traditions such as Quimbanda don't think twice before helping people break up marriages or to eliminate competitors, but many Neo-Pagans and Wiccans and also Christian readers don't want to compromise their sense of right and wrong in dealing with clients. Don't force your belief system on others, but simply decline or refer your clients to someone else if you feel that a request brought to you is inappropriate.

Take care of yourself first! Your family and your own health should be your first priority! As a fortune teller and card reader, I have yet to experience a situation of life and death for one of my clients. True, people's problems and needs are real and by offering your services as a reader, you also take on the responsibility to advise and help your clients. But in all this, never forget that your own life has to come first. Don't neglect your family and your personal life for helping others. A burned out reader, who's life is chaotic and in upheaval is no help to anyone. If your life is in such a state at the moment or if you ever encounter a situation where you need to take care of your own problems first, then take a break from reading for others and straighten your own problems out first. Prevention is always better then healing, so try not to let it come that far! Part III will also give some more information on spiritual protection and contains tips and tricks on how to keep your own life on track.

All in all, have fun and enjoy The Game of Destiny!

THE CARDS

1 – The Cavalier
Nine of Hearts

General Meaning

The Cavalier is generally a good card. It indicates good news, important messages and nice surprises brought to the client. This news can come from a faraway place within the country where the client lives or from a different country. In our time, The Cavalier can also represent a car or motorbike. In relation to love and relationships, The Cavalier indicates new romance. Speaking of employment and occupation, this card speaks of new chances and lucrative offers. Recovery from illnesses and new hope is offered in relation to health. When using the Great Spread (page 143), the card above The Cavalier usually shows the clients dreams and hopes whilst the surrounding cards give information on real-life scenarios.

Combinations

The Cavalier + The Clover

General Good News

The Cavalier + The Ship

Getting ready for a new beginning. Depending on the surrounding cards, this can also indicate overseas relations and foreign languages

The Cavalier + The House

Good news related to the home/coming to the home

The Cavalier + The Tree

Progression in Life

The Cavalier + The Clouds

The strength to clear one's life

The Cavalier + The Snake

Progress is made in an unexpected and delayed fashion

The Cavalier + The Coffin

Stagnation

The Cavalier + The Flowers

Arrival, visitors, presents

The Cavalier + The Scythe

Unexpected visitors, spontaneous projects

The Cavalier + The Whip

New contacts, talks, contracts

The Cavalier + The Birds

Decisions between two possible courses of action, unsure news

The Cavalier + The Child

The client is/was the bearer of news

The Cavalier + The Fox

Wrong or misleading news/information

The Cavalier + The Bear

News from/by/related to an older person

The Cavalier + The Star

Work done/performed at night

The Cavalier + The Stork

A change of direction

The Cavalier + The Dog

Projects done with the help of Friends

The Cavalier + The Tower

Thinking about separation, changes and relocation

The Cavalier + The Garden

A gathering/party/ball

The Cavalier + The Mountain

Progression and relief after hard times or blockages are eliminated.

The Cavalier + The Ways

Going in the right direction, following the right course of action

The Cavalier + The Mouse

Leaving all negativity and 'baggage' behind and moving on

The Cavalier + The Heart

Being able to progress easily. The path of the heart

The Cavalier + The Ring

Breaking free, release (also coming out of jail)

The Cavalier + The Book

Movements related to documents and paperwork

The Cavalier + The Letter

Written messages (letters/emails/notes)

The Cavalier + The Gentleman

A young man, active, sportive and full of self-esteem

The Cavalier + The Lady

A young woman, active, sportive and full of self-esteem

The Cavalier + The Lily

Family engagements and endeavors

The Cavalier + The Sun

Strength, being able to proceed with enough energy backup

The Cavalier + The Moon

Nightly activities

The Cavalier + The Key

Positive news will surely come

The Cavalier + The Fishes

Monetary increase or gain

The Cavalier + The Anchor

Stable relationships and/or partnerships

The Cavalier + The Cross

Sorrows

2 – The Clover
Six of Diamonds

General Meaning

The Clover is a card of happiness. It shows that something positive will happen soon. It is generally called the card of 'small luck' - compared to The Sun, which is seen as 'big luck'. The Clover also shows positive conclusions to all ventures and projects. In relation to love and relationships, The Clover indicates harmony and general 'good times'. Speaking of employment and occupation, this card tells the client that long deserved rewards are on the way. A quick and almost miraculous recovery is promised in relation to health.

Combinations

The Clover + The Cavalier

Small success

The Clover + The Ship

A short trip, not too far away

The Clover + The House

Happiness and luck at home, good news coming to the house

The Clover + The Tree

Long-lasting happiness

The Clover + The Clouds

Positive changes. Negative and unpleasantness leaves

The Clover + The Snake

Positive changes after struggles and previous wrong turns

The Clover + The Coffin

A phase of rest, but also tiredness and uneasiness

The Clover + The Flowers

Happiness

The Clover + The Scythe

Sudden luck

The Clover + The Whip

Discussions and a hasty exchange of words

The Clover + The Birds

A string of luck

The Clover + The Child

Small, little luck

The Clover + The Fox

It looks like luck, but turns out not to be

The Clover + The Bear

Diplomacy is needed for a short time

The Clover + The Star

Dreams and ideas

The Clover + The Stork

Positive changes

The Clover + The Dog

Short-lived friendship

The Clover + The Tower

Boundaries

The Clover + The Garden

Sudden invitations to parties or other social events

The Clover + The Mountain

Short-lived blockages

The Clover + The Ways

Short distances

The Clover + The Mouse

Troubles

The Clover + The Heart

Joy and happiness in matters of the heart (love and romance)

The Clover + The Ring

Short-lived relationships and/or co-operations

The Clover + The Book

A positive or pleasant secret

The Clover + The Letter

Short-lived contacts

The Clover + The Gentleman

It will happen soon

The Clover + The Lady

It will happen soon

The Clover + The Lily

Happy family

The Clover + The Sun

Short strength and power

The Clover + The Moon

Short-lived recognition

The Clover + The Key

You will soon know when/you found out 'over night'

The Clover + The Fishes

Short-lived money

The Clover + The Anchor

Short-lived work and employment, also temping or contracting

The Clover + The Cross

Happy endings

3 – The Ship
Ten of Spades

General Meaning

The Ship indicates travel and changes, but also relocation and migration. This can be seen as actual or emotional. Even though the client might not actually travel or relocate, he or she dreams and fantasizes about it. On a deeper level, this card talks about the subconscious mind, about hopes, longings and nostalgia as well as the desire to change and to break free. The Ship can also indicate foreigners or people of different nationality and/or complexion. In relation to love and relationships, The Ship indicates that already existing relationships will grow deeper. Speaking of employment and occupation, this card tells the client that he or she should carefully re-evaluate his or her course of actions. Speaking of health, this card advises the client to look for the 'real' problems behind illness and sickness.

Combinations

The Ship + The Cavalier

A trip by sea that also entails excursions on land

The Ship + The Clover

Travel will happen soon/has happened not long ago

The Ship + The House

Traveling home

The Ship + The Tree

An important, eventful journey (the person's destiny)

The Ship + The Clouds

A journey shrouded in mystery, possibly dodgy and dubious

The Ship + The Snake

Delayed journeys, also journeys and travels that are **not** direct or straight forward

The Ship + The Whip

Travels and journeys are being discussed

The Ship + The Birds

Two journeys, also journeys with different purposes

The Ship + The Child

A short journey with no particular destination

The Ship + The Fox

Unsuccessful journeys

The Ship + The Bear

A difficult journey

The Ship + The Star

Traveling north

The Ship + The Stork

Change of travel plans

The Ship + The Dog

Traveling to see friends (also, meeting friends on a journey)

The Ship + The Tower

Travels close to the border of the country

The Ship + The Garden

Traveling with people

The Ship + The Mountain

Journeys are blocked

The Ship + The Ways

Going in different directions

The Ship + The Mouse

Travel plans are not coming to pass

The Ship + The Heart

An important journey connected to matters of the heart

The Ship + The Ring

Journey by bus

The Ship + The Book

Unknown journey shrouded in secrecy. Also, winning travel tickets

The Ship + The Letter

News from far away

The Ship + The Gentleman

The client's partner lives far away

The Ship + The Lady

The client's partner lives far away

The Ship + The Lily

Traveling with family

The Ship + The Sun

Traveling south

The Ship + The Moon

Success following a journey

The Ship + The Key

Journey will sure happen

The Ship + The Fishes

Journey or travels connected to money

The Ship + The Anchor

Journey or travels connected to the client's job

The Ship + The Cross

Destined travels (this journey is meant to happen)

4 – The House
King of Hearts

General Meaning

Just as the card itself says, The House speaks of the person's own house and home. More information on the client's domestic life can be obtained from the surrounding cards. Additionally, this card tells the client that he or she should 'think big' and make plans for the distant future and not simply be satisfied with small success. The House also indicates stable relationships. In relation to health, the client can expect to soon recover from all ailments. Questioned about employment, this card indicates managerial positions and/or promotions.

Combinations

The House + The Cavalier

Stables (horses)

The House + The Clover

Luck is coming to the house

The House + The Ship

Houseboat

The House + The Tree

Good and stable health

The House + The Clouds

Problems are disappearing

The House + The Snake

Unconventional and unusual ways of finding a House (see the surrounding cards for more information)

The House + The Coffin

Retirement Home

The House + The Flowers

Parties at the home

The House + The Scythe

Commotion concerning the home (in same cases eviction)

The House + The Whip

Moving House

The House + The Birds

Second home

The House + The Child

New home

The House + The Fox

The wrong house

The House + The Bear

Secure and stable home (also the client's old home)

The House + The Star

Positive House

The House + The Stork

Changes at home, preparing to move

The House + The Dog

A good and secure house/home

The House + The Tower

Away from home

The House + The Garden

A large house or public building/skyscraper

The House + The Mountain

Problems related to a house

The House + The Ways

Secure and stable home, even though other areas of the client's life are affected with troubles

The House +The Mouse

Loss of house and home

The House + The Heart

The client's heart is attached to the house/home

The House + The Ring

Long lasting stability in the home (also long lasting and stable marriage)

The House + The Book

Documents related to the house and home (eg. House deeds, tenancy/lease agreements)

The House + The Letter

Money matters related to the client's own home

The House + The Gentleman

The home owner

The House + The Lady

The Lady of the House

The House + The Lily

Property belonging to the family

The House + The Sun

Summer house/holiday home

The House + The Moon

A house nearby the client's home

The House + The Key

A house/home ready to move into

The House + The Fishes

Bank

The House + The Anchor

The client enjoys home life and being at home

The House + The Cross

Hospital

5 – The Tree
Seven of Hearts

General Meaning

This card is called The Tree of Life by many readers. It symbolizes stability, steadfastness and rest. Depending on the surrounding cards, it can also indicate laziness or boredom. The tree tells us that it might take some time before we reach our goals. Even though we are on the right path, we still need to invest more time and lay a more stable foundation before we can reap the rewards of our work. The Tree also indicated stable and long-lasting love and relationships, excellent health and stable employment.

Combinations

The Tree + The Cavalier

Thirst for life

The Tree + The Clover

Perfect happiness and luck in life

The Tree + The Ship

Life's journeys

The Tree + The House

A deep connection with the home (family and native country)

The Tree + The Clouds

Sickness/diseases pass away quickly

The Tree + The Snake

Being set free from addictions and restrictions

The Tree + The Coffin

Psychological stress leads to physical illnesses

The Tree + The Flowers

The zest of life

The Tree + The Scythe

Danger of losing life

The Tree + The Whip

Discussions about life (also, counseling and psychotherapy)

The Tree + The Birds

Mood swings (either the client's own mood or being exposed to other people's mood swings)

The Tree + The Child

A new phase in life begins/began

The Tree + The Fox

The client is not living his or her life the way they should be

The Tree + The Bear

The client's past

The Tree + The Star

A spiritual house (church, spiritual centre, witches' coven, temple)

The Tree + The Stork

Changes in life

The Tree + The Dog

Life-long friendship

The Tree + The Tower

Isolation, a lonely life

The Tree + The Garden

A stable life in the public eye

The Tree + The Mountain

A life full off trials and tribulations (also, barriers in life and slow progress)

The Tree + The Ways

A period of 2 or more years

The Tree + The Mouse

Physical illnesses (not caused by the client's mental state or stress)

The Tree + The Heart

A happy life, filled with love

The Tree + The Ring

Lifelong relationship

The Tree + The Book

Well kept old secrets in life

The Tree + The Letter

Very important news with far reaching effects

The Tree + The Gentleman

Life partner

The Tree + The Lady

Life partner

The Tree + The Lily

Strong family ties

The Tree + The Sun

Excellent health

The Tree + The Moon

Depressive tendencies

The Tree + The Key

Destiny/life path

The Tree + The Fishes

A blurred and confusing situation

The Tree + The Anchor

The perfect job

The Tree + The Cross

Physical death

6 – The Clouds
King of Clubs

General Meaning

The meaning of The Clouds always depends on the position of the card in the game. Generally speaking we say that cards on the right of The Clouds show danger, fear and darkness whilst cards to the left show relief from and betterment of a situation. No matter which position the card takes, the client is always advised to be cautious and to tread carefully. No risks should be taken in any of the areas this card influences. Interpreting this card on a deeper level, The Clouds speak of the soul. The surrounding cards can therefore point out what the client's mental state is and what the client currently has on his or her mind. In relation to love and relationships, The Clouds speak of uncertainties and a small crisis. Questioned about work and employment, this card usually indicates hardship and stress. The Clouds can also speak of the danger of catching viruses and diseases which should not be taken lightly. Especially the lungs and respiratory system needs protection at this time.

Combinations

The Clouds + The Cavalier

Uncertainties

The Clouds + The Clover

Uncertainties and negativity lasting a short while

The Clouds + The Ship

An uncertain journey (it is not yet defined when and where the client will travel to)

The Clouds + The House

Negativity in the home

The Clouds + The Tree

Prone to sickness

The Clouds + The Snake

Suicidal tendencies, loss, negative influences

The Clouds + The Coffin

Prolonged sickness

The Clouds + The Flower

The outcome is not yet clear

The Clouds + The Scythe

Unpleasant surprises

The Clouds + The Whip

Discussions and talks – the client is advised to watch his words carefully

The Clouds + The Birds

Unsure which direction to take

The Clouds + The Child

Abortion

The Clouds + The Fox

Split personality, also diseases of the throat and respiratory system

The Clouds + The Bear

Instability

The Clouds + The Star

Dream world

The Clouds + The Stork

Negative changes

The Clouds + The Dog

Dubious friend, also loss of a friendship

The Clouds + The Tower

Restrictions

The Clouds + The Garden

Keeping company with shady people

The Clouds + The Mountain

Unclear hindrances

The Clouds + The Ways

Unclear decisions and choices

The Clouds + The Mouse

Severe sickness

The Clouds + The Heart

Heartache, lovesickness, uncertainty in matters of love

The Clouds + The Ring

Unclear relationships

The Clouds + The Book

Uncertainty, secrecy

The Clouds + The Letter

Unclear and uncertain news

The Clouds + The Gentleman

Many secrets and uncertainties in relationships

The Clouds + The Lady

Many secrets and uncertainties in relationships

The Clouds + The Lily

Sexually transmitted diseases, also diseases of the lower abdomen

The Clouds + The Sun

Weakened energy

The Clouds + The Moon

Worries/ups and downs

The Clouds + The Key

Lack of independence, also lack of confidence

The Clouds + The Fishes

Uncertainty in financial matters, possible financial loss

The Clouds + The Anchor

Unemployment, uncertain changes at the workplace

The Clouds + The Cross

Uncertainty in matters of health, danger of severe sickness

More information on **The Clouds** can be found on page 137.

7 – The Snake
Queen of Clubs

General Meaning

This card usually brings a warning and tells the client that he or she should be careful not to lose sight of his or her goals. It is very easy for the client at the moment to lose track of his or her plans. The Snake card warns the client not to take any shortcuts and not to make hasty choices in matters of love, money or general business, as these might only bring unwanted entanglements and confusion. Speaking about love and romance, this card indicates seduction and temptation but also the intrusion of another person into an existing relationship. Regarding health and wellbeing, this card tells the client that he or she needs to take better care of his or her health and to not so easily dismiss sickness. In matters of work and employment this card can also indicate the beneficial influence of an older woman. This however needs to be confirmed by the surrounding cards. The Snake is most often interpreted as danger and betrayal and warns the client of a woman near him or her which should be handled with care. Under normal circumstances, this woman would be middle aged and a rival to the client.

Combinations

The Snake + The Cavalier

Progress is made in an unexpected and delayed fashion (can also indicate that the client is thinking about a female person)

The Snake + The Clover

Unclear circumstances

The Snake + The Ship

Delayed journeys (also traffic jam, congestion)

The Snake + The House

Delays in coming home

The Snake + The Tree

The client's spine

The Snake + The Clouds

A woman with negative or 'strange vibes'

The Snake + The Coffin

Stagnation

The Snake + The Flowers

A young woman, also a group/party of woman

The Snake + The Scythe

A dangerous woman (we would also warn the client to be careful when going around corners and curbs as he or she is in danger of accidents on these areas*)

The Snake + The Whip

Discussions and talks are not what they should be (not speaking openly, falsehood)

The Snake + The Birds

The 'gift of the gab' – being able to talk oneself in or out of any situation

The Snake + The Child

The end of naivety

The Snake + The Fox

A trustworthy woman

The Snake + The Bear

Stability after struggles

The Snake + The Star

Clarity through unexpected news

The Snake + The Stork

Changes will not happen as quickly as anticipated

The Snake + The Dog

A short-lived friendship

The Snake + The Tower

Teaching ones goals after struggles

---

*This interpretation really falls under the Macumba section. See page 158 onwards

The Snake + The Garden

Things are prolonged as too many people know about them (keep your secrets more secret)

The Snake + The Mountain

There are no other possibilities – it will take time

The Snake + The Ways

Avoiding alternative possibilities/roads

The Snake + The Mouse

Fear consumes you

The Snake + The Heart

Visited by a woman

The Snake + The Ring

Unbreakable connections

The Snake + The Book

Secrecy

The Snake + The Letter

Delayed messages (news will reach the client indirect)

The Snake + The Gentleman

A false woman (be wary with this woman)

The Snake + The Lady

Female friends

The Snake + The Lily

Twisted family relations

The Snake + The Sun

New strength and energy from unexpected sources

The Snake + The Moon

Recognition

The Snake + The Key

Undesirable involvements/involvements causing trouble and headaches

The Snake + The Fishes

Shifting money around

The Snake + The Anchor

Sneakiness can secure projects

The Snake + The Cross

Grief

8 – The Coffin
Nine of Diamonds

General Meaning

The Coffin card usually shows that there is loss and imbalance in the client's life. This card can either indicate that sickness is near or that the client's health will at present not improve. Speaking on a deeper lever, this card also tells the client that unhealthy habits and situations need to come to a closure and that he or she can not continue the same way they have been going. A change of direction, ideas and attitude might be needed as the client is literally 'on the wrong path'. Speaking of love and relationships, this card tells the client that he or she is 'running out of luck' and that the end of a relationship could be unavoidable. Competition at work will also bring hardship and unnecessary complications. The Coffin also points towards issues with the client's physical heart and spine and he or she needs to take better care of these areas of his or her body.

Combinations

The Coffin + The Cavalier

Stagnation, projects have come to a stand-still

The Coffin + The Clover

A short pause, delays

The Coffin + The Ship

A break on a journey

The Coffin + The House

Sickness at home

The Coffin + The Tree

Tiredness, exhaustion

The Coffin + The Clouds

Sickness and diseases will pass

The Coffin + The Snake

Materialistic personality

The Coffin + The Flower

Healing/relief from sickness

The Coffin + The Scythe

Suddenly (what exactly happens suddenly is determined by the surrounding cards)

The Coffin + The Whip

Separation (what separates is determined by the surrounding cards)

The Coffin + The Birds

Double loss

The Coffin + The Child

Something new is about to start

The Coffin + The Fox

Stubbornness (the matter at hand is not being understood)

The Coffin + The Bear

Patience is needed

The Coffin + The Star

Listen to your intuition (blessings of the ancestors*)

The Coffin + The Stork

Changes will happen

The Coffin + The Dog

No contact between friends – the friendship rests/is put on ice

The Coffin + The Tower

Isolation and separation

The Coffin + The Garden

Abandoned building

The Coffin + The Mountain

Healing is blocked

---

*This second interpretation really falls under the Macumba section. See page 158 onwards

The Coffin + The Ways

Venereal diseases

The Coffin + The Mouse

Diseases of the Stomach and Digestive System

The Coffin + The Heart

Lovesickness (also, diseases of the heart)

The Coffin + The Ring

Divorce, love-relationships come to an end

The Coffin + The Book

Sickness that is not a real disease

The Coffin + The Letter

Sick notes (being signed off work for sickness)

The Coffin + The Gentleman

Stagnation and powerlessness will be released

The Coffin + The Lady

Female diseases

The Coffin + The Lily

Sadness and grief within the family

The Coffin + The Sun

Weakness

The Coffin + The Moon

Unsuccessfulness

The Coffin + The Key

Complete stagnation

The Coffin + The Fishes

Money is returned that was believed to be completely lost

The Coffin + The Anchor

Undertaker (also Exu Sete Cruzes and other Exus of the cemetery*)

The Coffin + The Cross

Total loss (not death though)

More information on **The Coffin** can be found on page 138.

*For further information on Exu see *Na Gira do Exu* by Mario dos Ventos, Lulu publishing, 2006.

9 – The Flowers
Queen of Spades

General Meaning

Called The Bouquet in *Petit Lenormand* deck, this card is by many readers seen as pointing towards people getting engaged and preparing for marriage. The card usually brings parties, family reunions and celebrations with it and can also indicate presents and gifts that the client will receive. Depending on the surrounding cards, The Flowers can also tell the client that he or she needs to use their charm and manners and not to engage in arguments to win in love and business. In relation to employment, this card tells the client that a nice, polite and charming woman will bring help and evolution to the client's workplace. This card also tells the client that his or her health will improve. Asking about actual diseases, The Flowers speak of growths and diseases of the skin.

Combinations

The Flowers + The Cavalier

Invitations and presents

The Flowers + The Clover

Friends and happiness

The Flowers + The Ship

A joyful journey

The Flowers + The House

Joy in the home

The Flowers + The Tree

Lasting happiness

The Flowers + The Clouds

Spontaneous/unexpected joy, happiness and surprises

The Flowers + The Snake

Naive, childlike person/personality

The Flowers + The Coffin

A nurse/nursing

The Flowers + The Scythe

Sudden surprises

The Flowers + The Whip

Congratulations

The Flowers + The Birds

Double invitations/two invitations

The Flowers + The Child

A young girl

The Flowers + The Fox

Having the facts wrong, gossip

The Flowers + The Bear

Friends in high places

The Flowers + The Star

Finding spirituality and the supernatural

The Flowers + The Stork

Pleasant change of location

The Flowers + The Dog

A good and pleasant friendship

The Flowers + The Tower

Practitioner of alternative medicine/Acupuncturist/Herbologist/Naturopathist

The Flowers + The Garden

Exhibitions

The Flowers + The Mountain

Boils or bumps on the head

The Flowers + The Ways

Searching for alternative possibilities and relief

The Flowers + The Mouse

It can not be stopped

The Flowers + The Heart

Positive developments in important matters

The Flowers + The Ring

Engagement (in relationships

The Flowers + The Book

Pleasant secrets that are not yet known

The Flowers + The Letter

Pleasant news (also, presents that are not of any material value)

The Flowers + The Gentleman

A man with two lovers

The Flowers + The Lady

A nice woman

The Flowers + The Lily

Family celebrations

The Flowers + The Sun

Pleasant developments

The Flowers + The Moon

The development of mediumistic abilities

The Flowers + The Key

A surprise for the client

The Flowers + The Fishes

A present of large material value

The Flowers + The Anchor

Pleasant relationships (not only speaking of matters of the heart but also business and friendships)

The Flowers + The Cross

Sudden endings, losses

10 – The Scythe
Jack of Diamonds

General Meaning

Similar to card number 6, The Clouds, The Scythe also needs to be interpreted mainly in relation to its position in the game. Cards to the left or before of The Scythe indicate danger from a particular situation or person. Cards to the right or after The Scythe warn that this particular danger is approaching faster then the client thinks. Cards underneath The Scythe speak of burdens brought into the client's life. This card usually tells the client to 'sit and wait' as this is not the time to make important decisions or to realize plans or projects. The Scythe warns the client of serious diseases and asks that he or she be exceptionally cautious with their health. Special care should be given to all soft and moist parts of the client's body. Speaking of love and relationships, the card tells the client that his or her relationship is in serious danger. The nature of the problem can be determined by the surrounding cards. In relation to work and employment, this card tells that the client might suffer from mobbing and that someone is trying to sabotage the client.

Combinations

The Scythe + The Cavalier

Scary but pleasant news

The Scythe + The Clover

Short-lived unpleasantness and shocks

The Scythe + The Ship

Travel by car or airplane

The Scythe + The House

Financial danger for the home

The Scythe + The Tree

Danger of life

The Scythe + The Clouds

Uncertainties clear up

The Scythe + The Snake

Careful with spinning machinery (cars, washing machines, tumble dryers - repairs may be needed)

The Scythe + The Coffin

Watch your head (feeding the head*)

The Scythe + The Flowers

Losses that will make room for something better

The Scythe + The Whip

Arguments (watch your tongue)

The Scythe + The Birds

Distress and turbulences

The Scythe + The Child

A small circle of people that should be treated with caution

The Scythe + The Fox

Danger from two sides (double danger)

The Scythe + The Bear

Dangerous passions

The Scythe + The Star

Mediumistic abilities are tainted by outside influences

The Scythe + The Stork

Dangerous changes

The Scythe + The Dog

An aggressive friend

The Scythe + The Tower

Sudden breakdown

The Scythe + The Garden

Keeping company with certain people can cause danger

---

*The 'feeding of the head' is a ceremony which can be performed by an initiate of African based traditions such as Umbanda, Candomble, Santeria or Vodou only. The client should if possible be sent to a priest of these religions for further investigation

The Scythe + The Mountain

Danger of bone fractions (also, tread carefully as positive and pleasant situations can turn into danger and unpleasantness)

The Scythe + The Ways

Dangerous roads and streets (literally speaking)

The Scythe + The Mouse

Diseases of the Stomach (careful with gluttony/over-eating)

The Scythe + The Heart

Jealousy (also High Blood Pressure)

The Scythe + The Ring

Dangerous relations (also danger for existing relationships)

The Scythe + The Book

Sudden secrets (also, Partner in Crime or negatively)

The Scythe + The Letter

Inspiring news

The Scythe + The Gentleman

An aggressive man

The Scythe + The Lady

An aggressive and hectic woman

The Scythe + The Lily

Passionate sex (also danger of rape and unwanted sexual intercourse)

The Scythe + The Sun

Explosions and exhaustion of personal strength

The Scythe + The Moon

Sadistic tendencies

The Scythe + The Key

Uncertainty will suddenly change into definite knowledge

The Scythe + The Fishes

No relations to money (no appreciation for money)

The Scythe + The Anchor

Stress at work, being overworked

The Scythe + The Cross

Sudden losses

More information on **The Scythe** can be found on page 138.

11 – The Whip
Jack of Clubs

General Meaning

Also called The Broom or in the *Petit Lenormand* deck The Rod, this card usually speaks of strife, worries and arguments and tells the client to keep a 'cool head' and not to lose his or her temper in dealing with other people. This can relate to love and relationships as well as work and employment. The Whip warns that plans and ideas are not thought through well enough and that the client should consult second opinion before he or she tried to manifest his or her ideas. In extreme cases, this card can also point towards entanglements with the law. Related to health, the card tells the client to take special care of his or her muscles, hands and upper limps but also of their nerves. Infections of the client's throat as well as speech impediments can also be an issue here.

Combinations

The Whip + The Cavalier

Swift, short communication

The Whip + The Clover

Quick but pleasant communication

The Whip + The Ship

Talks about travel

The Whip + The House

Talks and discussions at home

The Whip + The Tree

Discussions drag on

The Whip + The Clouds

Talks will resolve unclear situations

The Whip + The Snake

Being articulate and eloquent

The Whip + The Coffin

Speechless

The Whip + The Flowers

Pleasant talks

The Whip + The Scythe

Strife

The Whip + The Birds

Meaningless discussions

The Whip + The Child

Childlike discussions

The Whip + The Fox

Two-faced talks (saying one thing, meaning another)

The Whip + The Bear

Layer or mediator

The Whip + The Star

Spiritual conversations (prayer)

The Whip + The Stork

Talks and discussions bring/cause changes

The Whip + The Dog

Comfort

The Whip + The Tower

Going to court, court hearings

The Whip + The Garden

Sudden discussions (also attending speeches, recitals)

The Whip + The Mountain

Blockages in discussions and talks (not getting through to someone, not being able to get the message across, not listening)

The Whip + The Ways

Using excuses

The Whip + The Mouse

Discussing losses

The Whip + The Heart

Strife with loved ones

The Whip + The Ring

Relationship problems

The Whip + The Book

Discussions and talks bring clarity

The Whip + The Letter

Short messages (also, a letter is returned)

The Whip + The Gentleman

An honest and intelligent man

The Whip + The Lady

A woman who understands completely

The Whip + The Lily

Clarity in personal matters (not work related)

The Whip + The Sun

Empowering talks and discussions

The Whip + The Moon

Success and acknowledgement comes from discussions and talks

The Whip + The Key

Discussions and talks will definitely happen

The Whip + The Fishes

Discussions and talks about money (financial matters)

The Whip + The Anchor

Discussions and talks about work and employment

The Whip + The Cross

Strife and unpleasant exchanges of words will end

12 – The Birds
Seven of Diamonds

General Meaning

Other editions of The Lenormand Deck call this card The Owls and show two owls sitting in a tree. The *Petit Lenormand* deck however lists this card as The Birds but shows two woman interacting with each other in business matters. This card tells the client to exercise wisdom and caution and shows that the client is very 'hot headed' and that he or she is able to create much havoc with their words and actions. The client is also easily influenced by people, listening to many different opinions and ideas without making up his or her own mind. This might create additional problems in their life. The Birds also tell the client to rethink their current plan of actions as continuing his or her ways will create more worries and anger then what it is worth. Speaking about love and relationships, this card speaks of much excitement for the client, which may create some mood swings. Related to work and employment, this card can point towards further education or additional training courses which the client should take.

Combinations

The Birds + The Cavalier

Doubts and upheaval

The Birds + The Clover

Short-lived doubts

The Birds + The Ship

Roundtrip (journeying to destination and then returning)

The Birds + The House

Two homes

The Birds + The Tree

Two people (either a couple or twins)

The Birds + The Clouds

Doubts and upheavals disappear

The Birds + The Snake

Dubious circumstances

The Birds + The Coffin

Insecurities disappear

The Birds + The Flowers

A double present (or two presents)

The Birds + The Scythe

Doubts disappear quickly

The Birds + The Whip

Discussions and talks with two parties/persons

The Birds + The Child

Two children of different ages

The Birds + The Fox

Honesty – uncertainties are eliminated

The Birds + The Bear

Role plays

The Birds + The Star

Dancing

The Birds + The Stork

Doubts about changes

The Birds + The Dog

Worries about a friend/friendship

The Birds + The Tower

Restrictions

The Birds + The Garden

Uncertainties in relation to public offices/governmental institutions

The Birds + The Mountain

Blockages bring insecurities

The Birds + The Ways

Finding the right course of action

The Birds + The Mouse

Worries and doubts

The Birds + The Heart

Nervousness (also heart problems)

The Birds + The Ring

Two connections (possibly two relationships)

The Birds + The Book

A double secret (a secret with two sides)

The Birds + The Letter

Two messages

The Birds + The Gentleman

Leaving uncertainties and fluctuations behind

The Birds + The Lady

Uncertainties and fluctuations

The Birds + The Lily

Doubtful relationships, insecurities within the family

The Birds + The Sun

Double power

The Birds + The Moon

Double success

The Birds + The Key

Uncertainties and doubts will definitely leave

The Birds + The Fishes

Money from two different sources

The Birds + The Anchor

Two jobs

The Birds + The Cross

Grief vanishes

13 – The Child
Jack of Spades

General Meaning

The Child speaks of naivety, new beginnings and dependencies. This card usually shows the client's own children, never grandchildren or other young members of the family. If this card appears directly above the Person Card, then this can indicate that the client is overly naïve and not 'clued up' with what's going on around him or her. Some readers will interpret this position as indicating that the client is lacking intelligence. The Child card also tells the client that he or she needs to be led more by their good judgment and intelligence and that he or she stop acting childish or immature. It also advised that the client should not trust or follow others blindly but to listen to his or her own intuition and better judgment. In relation to love and relationships, this card tells the client that their love life is not yet stable and still has to grow and mature. If questioned about health, this card tells us that the client is steadily improving. New beginnings and business ventures are also about to take shape.

Combinations

The Child + The Cavalier

New projects

The Child + The Clover

Brief meetings/encounters (spending little time together)

The Child + The Ship

A short trip

The Child + The House

Joyful parties/meetings at home

The Child + The Tree

A new (phase of) life

The Child + The Clouds

Starting over again

The Child + The Snake

Feeling of powerlessness vanishes

The Child + The Coffin

Delays with new projects

The Child + The Flowers

Children's party

The Child + The Scythe

Disturbance related to a child or new projects vanish

The Child + The Whip

Immaturity (literally 'not coming out of puberty')

The Child + The Birds

News bring clarity (knowing which one of two options to take)

The Child + The Fox

The wrong child (as in 'adopting the wrong child' or 'getting custody over the wrong child')

The Child + The Bear

Childlike trust

The Child + The Star

Purity

The Child + The Stork

Change of place (but not far away)

The Child + The Dog

Two friends of different age

The Child + The Tower

An only child (also, large age gap between siblings)

The Child + The Garden

Kindergarten (UK: nursery, pre-school)

The Child + The Mountain

Stubbornness vanishes

The Child + The Ways

Small escape route

The Child + The Mouse

Small losses

The Child + The Heart

Naivety

The Child + The Ring

Relationships/projects need to be worked on

The Child + The Book

A secret related to a child

The Child + The Letter

Small messages

The Child + The Gentleman

A young man

The Child + The Lady

A woman that is closely connected to a child (does not have to be her own child)

The Child + The Lily

A small family

The Child + The Sun

New beginnings with much energy and strength/courage

The Child + The Moon

Sensitive child

The Child + The Key

New beginnings are definitely on the way

The Child + The Fishes

A small amount of money (also, a monetary tip)

The Child + The Anchor

A small job (also, not much work)

The Child + The Cross

Small troubles and worries vanish

14 – The Fox
Nine of Clubs

General Meaning

The Fox speaks of lies, betrayal, sneakiness and double meanings and always warns the client to be cautious of losses. This being said, depending on its position in the game, The Fox can also challenge the client to be more forthright, honest and appreciative. If this card appears either to the left or above the Person Card, then this indicates that the client is nosy and easily mistrusts others. Showing to the right of the Person Card, it points towards dishonesty and lies. If however it appears 'in the back' of the Person Card - either to the left of The Gentleman (card 28) or to the right of The Lady (card 29) - then it shows that the client is very secretive. If questioned about love and relationships, The Fox warns that the client's partner is dishonest and that the client is being cheated. Nothing is as it seems! In relation to work and employment, this card tells the client that he or she needs to be careful with intrigues at the workplace. Heath issues are also not as they seem and the client should consult a second physician for an additional opinion on his or her particular case.

Combinations

The Fox + The Cavalier

News that can be trusted

The Fox + The Clover

Sudden/unexpected money (also, making money quickly)

The Fox + The Ship

A positive journey will happen shortly/has happened not long ago

The Fox + The House

Positive changes in legal matters related to the house

The Fox + The Tree

Danger of life will pass

The Fox + The Clouds

Uncertain/'cloudy' circumstances are cleared up

The Fox + The Snake

A false, two-faced woman

The Fox + The Coffin

Being too open for everything

The Fox + The Flowers

Honesty

The Fox + The Scythe

Sudden/completely unexpected surprises

The Fox + The Whip

Willfully giving the wrong information

The Fox + The Birds

Saying one thing, meaning another

The Fox + The Child

Caring for something or someone for the wrong reasons

The Fox + The Bear

Furry pets (such as cats or dogs, but not birds or reptiles)

The Fox + The Star

Wrong medication

The Fox + The Stork

Wrong changes

The Fox + The Dog

A completely honest and trustworthy friend

The Fox + The Tower

The client needs to find another physician for his or her medical problems (consulting a specialist)

The Fox + The Garden

Trustworthy company

The Fox + The Mountain

Change of attitude and behavior for the better

The Fox + The Ways

Moving in the right direction/being 'on the right path'

The Fox + The Mouse

Danger of thieves and robbers

The Fox + The Heart

Showing kindness and affection for the wrong reasons

The Fox + The Ring

Wrong contracts and relationships (not just in matters of the heart)

The Fox + The Book

Wrong documents

The Fox + The Letter

Honest messages

The Fox + The Gentleman

Telling the truth

The Fox + The Lady

Lies

The Fox + The Lily

Wrong attitudes towards the family

The Fox + The Sun

Using energy and strength for the wrong reasons

The Fox + The Moon

Wrong/false ideas and preconceptions

The Fox + The Key

Mistakes

The Fox + The Fishes

Clever with money/investments/spending

The Fox + The Anchor

Intrigues at the workplace

The Fox + The Cross

Burdens are lifted (having been burdened for the wrong reasons)

15 – The Bear

Ten of Clubs

General Meaning

The Bear brings power, strength and trust to the consultation and in most cases symbolizes a male person in the client's life. This card tells the client that he or she is on the right path and should not change track at this point in time. Enough resources are available to the client and he or she should trust in their own abilities to see their plans, hopes and dreams come true. Questioned about love and relationships, this card tells the client that he or she has found a good, strong and reliable partner in life. In relation to work and employment, The Bear tells the client that he or she should set him or herself high goals and work towards them as their ambition will be rewarded. Health issues are also improving as the client gathers inner strength.

Combinations

The Bear + The Cavalier

Projects and activities gain stability

The Bear + The Clover

Short-lived stability

The Bear + The Ship

A journey without problems

The Bear + The House

Stable home/comfort

The Bear + The Tree

Steadfastness (also 'love of nature')

The Bear + The Clouds

Not giving room to uncertainties

The Bear + The Snake

Everything is stable (also 'everyone is working together for the same ends')

The Bear + The Coffin

Problems can not cause harm

The Bear + The Flowers

Being charming and attentive

The Bear + The Scythe

Stability is gained quickly/suddenly

The Bear + The Whip

A lawyer

The Bear + The Birds

Stability, no matter which choices are made or which course of action is chosen

The Bear + The Child

Fatherly support (not necessarily from the client's father though)

The Bear + The Fox

Fur and animal skins

The Bear + The Star

Intuition (also Guiding Spirits*)

The Bear + The Stork

A change of place/location

The Bear + The Dog

Friendship without compromises

The Bear + The Tower

A person 'in high places'/a very important person

The Bear + The Garden

The head of an organization/a patron

The Bear + The Mountain

Stubbornness (also, not accepting other people's opinions)

---

*This second interpretation really falls under the Macumba section. See page 158 onwards

The Bear + The Ways

Willingness to make compromises

The Bear + The Mouse

Some minor problems with stability

The Bear + The Heart

Passionate love (also jealousy)

The Bear + The Ring

Stable relationships

The Bear + The Book

A secretive person

The Bear + The Letter

A public person as intermediater (such as police or social workers)

The Bear + The Gentleman

One of the parents is ruling/influencing the client's life

The Bear + The Lady

One of the parents is ruling/influencing the client's life

The Bear + The Lily

The head of the family (also the oldest member of the family)

The Bear + The Sun

Determination

The Bear + The Moon

An influential person (also, a high ranking member of a spiritual religion/tradition)

The Bear + The Key

The highest authority at the workplace

The Bear + The Fishes

An official person who deals with money (banker, security services, payroll)

The Bear + The Anchor

Working for the government (local or national)

The Bear + The Cross

A high ranking person (also, a person on whom many honors have been bestowed, a cleric, bishop, high priest)

16 – The Star
Six of Hearts

General Meaning

The Star is seen as a card of the arts, music, sensitivity, inner clarity and refinement. When this card appears, it tells the client that he or she will be successful in his or her endeavors. Little is needed for the client to achieve the goals he or she has set. Love and relationships are developing well and bring much fulfillment into the client's life. All questions and doubts related to work and employment will be eliminated and the client will be able to proceed with much clarity. However, The Star also advises the client to take better care of his or her health by developing a better rest and sleeping pattern.

Combinations

The Star + The Cavalier

Receiving messages from the spirit world (not directly but via other people)

The Star + The Clover

Quick intuition (intuition does not last very long)

The Star + The Ship

Daydreams

The Star + The House

Mediumistic house (also a Spirit Medium)

The Star + The Tree

Life dedicated to spirituality

The Star + The Clouds

Drug abuse

The Star + The Snake

A female medium

The Star + The Coffin

Spiritual disturbances/negative interferences from the spirit world

The Star + The Flowers

Herbal medicine (also Rootworkers, Hoodoo practices)

The Star + The Scythe

Sudden insights

The Star + The Whip

Dowsing

The Star + The Birds

Precise messages from different mediumistic sources/people

The Star + The Child

Spiritual development

The Star + The Fox

Negative influences

The Star + The Bear

The client's Guardian Angel

The Star + The Stork

Changes will bring positive developments

The Star + The Dog

Deep friendship/soul mates

The Star + The Tower

A doctor/physician

The Star + The Garden

Theater

The Star + The Mountain

Memory losses

The Star + The Ways

Clear goals

The Star + The Mouse

Loss of clarity

The Star + The Heart

Deep love

The Star + The Ring

Relationships bring luck

The Star + The Book

Suspicions and ideas about a secret are correct

The Star + The Letter

Contacting the spirit world/séances

The Star + The Gentleman

An intelligent, open-hearted man with mediumistic abilities

The Star + The Lady

An intelligent, open-hearted man with mediumistic abilities

The Star + The Lily

Faithfulness (also, an open and honest relationship)

The Star + The Sun

Clairvoyance (opening the '3rd eye')

The Star + The Moon

Telepathy

The Star + The Key

Mediumistic abilities that are not yet developed

The Star + The Fishes

Spiritual connections between two people

The Star + The Anchor

Karmic connections

The Star + The Cross

The client's destiny

More information in **The Star** can be found on page 139.

17 – The Stork
Queen of Hearts

General Meaning

The Stork is the card of change. The nature of these changes either positive or negative, can only be seen from the surrounding cards. We usually say that the card to the left of The Stork brings what is shown after The Stork. Special attention needs to be taken when The Stork appears in a constellation with **The Tower** (card 19) and with the dark part of **The Clouds** (card 6). This usually indicates legal matters, law enforcement towards the client and in extreme cases jail or other types of persecution. Questioned on its own and related to health however, this card always tells the client that his or her health problems are over.

Combinations

The Stork + The Cavalier

Changes (also news from two different sources)

The Stork + The Clover

Changes that need quick actions

The Stork + The Ship

Moving home twice – one close to the original residence, the second further away

The Stork + The House

Moving home once

The Stork + The Tree

Planned changes are not happening as planned

The Stork + The Clouds

Thinking about changes but no concrete plans have been made

The Stork + The Snake

Many hurdles have to be overcome to see changes come to pass

The Stork + The Coffin

Changes are not at all possible

The Stork + The Flower

Happiness brings changes

The Stork + The Scythe

Hectic change of location (has to be done very quickly)

The Stork + The Whip

Punishment (also Court of Law, Jail)

The Stork + The Birds

Two options/possibilities for change

The Stork + The Child

Pregnancy

The Stork + The Fox

Changes should not happen at this time

The Stork + The Bear

Changes bring firmness and stability

The Stork + The Star

Change will be good (supported by the spirit world)

The Stork + The Dog

Positive changes in a friendship

The Stork + The Tower

Limited changes

The Stork + The Garden

Changes in the client's social life

The Stork + The Mountain

Changes are stopped

The Stork + The Ways

Resisting changes (taking the easiest way out)

The Stork + The Mouse

Changes bring loss

The Stork + The Heart

Changes in matters of the heart (not just love and relationships but also in areas that are of special importance and interest to the client)

The Stork + The Ring

Marriage through love

The Stork + The Book

Changes that are not yet known/that are still kept secret

The Stork + The Letter

News about changes

The Stork + The Gentleman

Changes brought by a man

The Stork + The Lady

Changes brought by a woman

The Stork + The Lily

New beginnings (also, new additions to the family)

The Stork + The Sun

Traveling south (or into warmer climates)

The Stork + The Moon

The way the client is seen by others will change/has changed

The Stork + The Key

Changes are bound to happen

The Stork + The Fishes

Positive financial changes (financial improvement)

The Stork + The Anchor

Stable changes (changes can not affect stability)

The Stork + The Cross

Pain and sufferings comes to an end

18 – The Dog
Ten of Hearts

General Meaning

The Dog is one of the most positive cards in the Lenormand Deck. It offers help and support and speaks of faithfulness, trust, stability and longevity. The Dog indicates a faithful friend, in most cases male. It tells the client that he or she has a friend in their life, who will support them in everything he or she does and that the client should not doubt this friends faithfulness. Questioned about love and relationships, this card tells the client that his or her partner truly loves and supports them and that their relationship is also a deep friendship. In relation to work and employment, The Dog tells the client that someone will give help and support for the client to succeed in his or her career. Speaking about health and wellbeing, this card also indicates that the client should not stop any treatments he or she is currently having.

Combinations

The Dog + The Cavalier

Making plans with friends

The Dog + The Clover

Short-lived friendship

The Dog + The Ship

Traveling with friends

The Dog + The House

Hospitality

The Dog + The Tree

Friends for life

The Dog + The Clouds

The beginning of a friendship

The Dog + The Snake

Making friends after problems are overcome

The Dog + The Coffin

'Sick' friendship (a friendship that is about to break)

The Dog + The Flower

A very good friend

The Dog + The Scythe

Exciting friendships

The Dog + The Whip

Friendly discussions

The Dog + The Birds

Friendship with many ups and downs

The Dog + The Child

Naïve friendship (also, a younger brother)

The Dog + The Fox

A false friend

The Dog + The Bear

A good natured and helpful friend (also, someone who is not very 'clued up with the world')

The Dog + The Star

Clear and honest friendship (also, spiritual bond between friends, friends who share the same spiritual path)

The Dog + The Stork

Changes in a friendship

The Dog + The Tower

Egoistic friendship

The Dog + The Garden

Friend who likes to be the center of attention (very sociable, outgoing friend)

The Dog + The Mountain

Friendship is momentarily blocked by stubbornness

The Dog + The Ways

Companionship

The Dog + The Mouse

Loss of a friend (end of a friendship)

The Dog + The Heart

Friendship filled with much love and appreciating for each other

The Dog + The Ring

A closely knit family (friends that are 'like brothers and sisters')

The Dog + The Book

Secret friendship

The Dog + The Letter

Superficial friendship

The Dog + The Gentleman

A male friend

The Dog + The Lady

A female friend

The Dog + The Lily

Friends of the family

The Dog + The Sun

Strong, lasting friendship

The Dog + The Moon

Soul mates (also, friends that are 'on the same wave length')

The Dog + The Key

Absolutely trustworthy and reliable friends

The Dog + The Fishes

Love of money (choosing money over friends)

The Dog + The Anchor

A stable friendship

The Dog + The Cross

Karmic friendship (people are destined to be friends)

19 – The Tower
Six of Spades

General Meaning

The Tower speaks of loneliness, isolation and separation but also of governmental offices and even foreign countries. When this card appears, it tells the client that his or her chosen path is not always comfortable and at times hard and energy consuming. The client should not expect much help from others at this point in time and needs to rely upon him or herself alone. The Tower more then any other card encourages the client to be strong and patient and to continue in the face if opposition. On a deeper level, this card also advises the client not to isolate him or herself emotionally as well as physically from others. In terms of love and relationships, this card tells the client to spend more time with his or her loved ones and especially with his or her partner to avoid further separation. Questioned about work and employment, this card usually indicates either a complete change of job, including possible relocation or changes and restructuring at the client's current workplace. Speaking in terms of health and wellbeing, The Tower warns of hidden diseases and infections.

Combinations

The Tower + The Cavalier
Leaving loneliness behind (breaking free)

The Tower + The Clover
Finding luck and happiness when alone

The Tower + The Ship
Traveling within the country (without crossing borders)

The Tower + The House

Two houses close to each other

The Tower + The Tree

A long life (more then 80 years)

The Tower + The Clouds

Uncertainties and restrictions disappear

The Tower + The Snake

The client's mother

The Tower + The Coffin

Hospital (can also be mental institution)

The Tower + The Flowers

A fenced garden (also a court yard garden)

The Tower + The Scythe

Electric power plant/power station

The Tower + The Whip

Court of law (also, serious conversations with the client's father)

The Tower + The Birds

Being worried about loneliness

The Tower + The Child

Boarding School (also, Orphanage)

The Tower + The Fox

Jail

The Tower + The Bear

The client's father

The Tower + The Star

Doctor of Medicine/a physician

The Tower + The Stork

Personal changes such as change of character (also withdrawals)

The Tower + The Dog

Separation between friends

The Tower + The Garden

A building with many visitors

The Tower + The Mountain

Blocked friendship

The Tower + The Ways

Temporary separation

The Tower + The Mouse

Separation and loss

The Tower + The Heart

Lonely hearted

The Tower + The Ring

Relationship brings restrictions

The Tower + The Book

A secret will not be revealed

The Tower + The Letter

News (from within the country but not from abroad or out of state)

The Tower + The Gentleman

Stubbornness

The Tower + The Lady

Being egotistical

The Tower +The Lily

Peace at home

The Tower + The Sun

Having double the amount of energy then usual

The Tower + The Moon

Isolating oneself

The Tower + The Key

Personal strength and energy are very much restricted

The Tower + The Fishes

Bank

The Tower + The Anchor

A factory

The Tower + The Cross

A cloister or monastery

20 – The Garden
Eight of Spades

General Meaning

Whereas The Flowers (card 9) speak of the engagement of two people, The Garden usually points towards marriage. This card also indicates parties, concerts, conferences and other public events and engagements. The Garden brings job, happiness and the realization of the client's dreams and hopes. If questioned in relation to work and employment, this card tells the client that his or her goals are almost reached. Speaking in terms of health, this card shows that the client is about to fully recover from past illnesses. However, pregnant woman who question the cards about the health and wellbeing of their unborn child should usually take this card as a sign that they should see a physician at their earliest convenience.

Combinations

The Garden + The Cavalier

Looking forward to attend a large event or party

The Garden + The Clover

Short-notice invitation to a public gathering

The Garden + The Ship

Traveling with many people (such as a cruise)

The Garden + The House

Large events such as balls or concerts (but also indoor markets and fairs)

The Garden + The Tree

A public park (also, living in the 'public eye')

The Garden + The Clouds

Uncertainties related to the public

The Garden + The Snake

Dodging your way through society

The Garden + The Coffin

Hospital

The Garden + The Flowers

Outdoor Exhibitions (such as Garden Shows)

The Garden + The Scythe

Unexpected invitations to large gatherings

The Garden + The Whip

Conferences, seminars

The Garden + The Birds

Two different events (also, events of different nature/purpose)

The Garden + The Child

Small events/gatherings

The Garden + The Fox

Betrayal (caution when meeting people at events/gatherings)

The Garden + The Bear

High-society events

The Garden + The Star

Theater, Movie theater (UK: Cinema)

The Garden + The Stork

Location-change for an event(s)

The Garden + The Dog

Meeting good friends, parties with good friends

The Garden + The Tower

Elite society (events/gatherings/parties are only open to selected individuals)

The Garden + The Mountain

Difficulties getting to/into events/gatherings/parties

The Garden + The Ways

Finding public alternatives

The Garden + The Mouse

Agoraphobia (feeling uncomfortable in public/crowds)

The Garden + The Heart

A helping hand (also unity, sticking together)

The Garden + The Ring

Wedding

The Garden + The Book

Public library

The Garden + The Letter

News related to public relations (also, elections, voting)

The Garden + The Gentleman

Not being interested in, or leaving certain parts of society behind

The Garden + The Lady

Looking for contacts, searching public approval

The Garden + The Lily

Charities and charitable events

The Garden + The Sun

Benefiting from attending events/gatherings/parties and also from keeping company with the right people

The Garden + The Moon

Events/gatherings/parties which bring recognition and self-esteem

The Garden + The Key

An event/gathering/party is certain to take place

The Garden + The Fishes

Events/gatherings/parties with emotional involvement (can be auctions, psychic fairs)

The Garden + The Anchor

Working with the public/in the public sector

The Garden + The Cross

Church/temple

21 – The Mountain
Eight of Clubs

General Meaning

The Mountain speaks of hindrances, frustration, and hurdles, but can also indicate stubbornness and reservation in the client's life. It usually warns that projects are not moving as quickly as they are meant to and that some extra energy and persuasiveness is needed to see plans and endeavors come to fruition. This can influence all areas of the client's life, from frustration in matters of love and relationship to work and employment. The client is advised to be more flexible and very diplomatic in presenting his or her ideas. Stubbornness will at this point in time only hinder the client's progress and might jeopardize his or her future. This card also warns the client not to be angry or bitter, as this could have serious effects on his or her health. In this aspect, The Mountain especially warns of Gall Stones and Kidney Stones.

Combinations

The Mountain + The Cavalier

Blocked thoughts and actions

The Mountain + The Clover

Short-lived blockages

The Mountain + The Ship

Blocked journeys/travels

The Mountain + The House

Hiding at home

The Mountain + The Tree

Blockages in life

The Mountain + The Clouds

Troubles

The Mountain + The Snake

Blockages are solved in unusual ways and are not straight-forward

The Mountain + The Coffin

A feeling of stagnation will be taken away

The Mountain + The Flowers

Problems and difficulties will easily be overcome

The Mountain + The Scythe

Problems will completely disappear in no time

The Mountain + The Whip

Discussions and talks are not happening/are blocked

The Mountain + The Birds

Not knowing which course of action to take

The Mountain + The Child

Stubbornness

The Mountain + The Fox

Underestimating problems and blockages

The Mountain + The Bear

An older person

The Mountain + The Star

A guiding spirit

The Mountain + The Stork

Changes are blocked

The Mountain + The Dog

Problems between friends

The Mountain + The Tower

Exceptional stubbornness

The Mountain + The Garden

Not being comfortable with getting too much attention

The Mountain + The Ways

Alternative roads are blocked

The Mountain + The Mouse

Inflexibility brings losses

The Mountain + The Heart

Blockages in matters of the heart

The Mountain + The Ring

Relationship is not developing as it should be

The Mountain + The Book

Secrets cause problems

The Mountain + The Letter

News is not reaching the recipient

The Mountain + The Gentleman

Leaving blockages behind

The Mountain + The Lady

Blocking oneself

The Mountain + The Lily

Blockages in/with the family

The Mountain + The Sun

Feeling drained

The Mountain + The Moon

Not being able to understand or make sense of

The Mountain + The Key

It is not meant to happen

The Mountain + The Fishes

Expected money is not coming in

The Mountain + The Anchor

Not being able to move forward with work/employment

The Mountain + The Cross

Blockages will be cleared

22 – The Ways
Queen of Diamonds

General Meaning

This card, even though called The Ways should be referred to as The Crossroads. It speaks of decisions and needed changes. The client is literally at a crossroad in his or her life but is, at this point in time, not able to make any firm decisions or commitments. No matter if questioned on love and relationships or work and employment, this card always indicates that the client is faced with difficult choices. He or she is searching for alternative possibilities and in extreme cases even escape roads. Additionally, if questioned on times or time frames, this card usually speaks of sequels of 7 - either 7 weeks or 7 months.

Combinations

The Ways + The Cavalier

Following the right course of acting brings fresh energy

The Ways + The Clover

Lucky escape roads

The Ways + The Ship

Journeys

The Ways + The House

Alternatives related to the house

The Ways + The Tree

A longer time period - at least 2 years

The Ways + The Clouds

Uncertain endings

The Ways + The Snake

Taking the 'long way round'

The Ways + The Coffin

Stagnation

The Ways + The Flowers

Enjoyable possibilities

The Ways + The Scythe

Sudden possibilities

The Ways + The Whip

Discussing goals and outcomes

The Ways + The Birds

Doubts vanish

The Ways + The Child

Moving forward without problems

The Ways + The Fox

The wrong direction

The Ways + The Bear

Moving forwards with stability

The Ways + The Star

Clear perspectives (knowing how to reach one's goals)

The Ways + The Stork

Constant changes

The Ways + The Dog

Enjoy doing what is needed

The Ways + The Tower

Breaking free from isolation

The Ways + The Garden

Projects/activities lead to large events (events/gatherings involving many people)

The Ways + The Mountain

Blockages vanish, moving forward with ease

The Ways + The Mouse

Alternative course of action brings loss

The Ways + The Heart

Making choices and planning the future based on love

The Ways + The Ring

The course of action brings closeness/relationship

The Ways + The Book

Two secrets projects/activities meet each other (also, coming together due to secrets)

The Ways + The Letter

Problems/Projects that need to/have been taken care of

The Ways + The Gentleman

Following the easiest course of action

The Ways + The Lady

Getting ready

The Ways + The Lily

Alternative course of action in dealing with family

The Ways + The Sun

Moving forward with much energy and strength

The Ways + The Moon

Reaching success and recognition

The Ways + The Key

It has to be done!

The Ways + The Fishes

Situations/activities involving money

The Ways + The Anchor

Versatility related to work

The Ways + The Cross

Situations/activities that can be handled and finished quickly

23 – The Mouse
Seven of Clubs

General Meaning

The Mouse card always speaks of loss. As with many other cards in the Lenormand Deck, the position of the card in the game can give more information of the area or areas in which the client should be especially careful of, in the near future. The card before or to the left of The Mouse shows what the client might be losing or has lost already. The card after or to the right of The Mouse however indicates what the client might lose as he or she is treating what is represented in this card very badly. Of special interest here is the combination of The Mouse with The Fishes (card 34) as this shows that the client is losing grip of his or her life and reality! The client is also warned to observe his or her behavior at the workplace as he or she might be watched and envied by others. Special care should also be taken in all areas of love and relationship. Even small problems and difficulties should be worked out immediately. The client's health might also be in danger and he or she is advised to take better care of their body.

Combinations

The Mouse + The Cavalier
What was lost will be returned

The Mouse + The Clover
Losing something/someone for a Short/temporary period

The Mouse + The Ship
Travel sickness

The Mouse + The House

Cleaning garbage/rubbish from the house/home (inside and outside)

The Mouse + The Tree

Negative situations and circumstances end

The Mouse + The Clouds

Depression and fear end

The Mouse + The Snake

Negativity/bad feelings related to a woman

The Mouse + The Coffin

Double loss of something/someone (if questioned on sickness: quick recovery)

The Mouse + The Flowers

Joy and pleasure turn into loss

The Mouse + The Scythe

What seemed lost is returned quickly

The Mouse + The Whip

Losing contact with people, not being able to reach a particular person

The Mouse + The Birds

Doubts are wiped out

The Mouse + The Child

Concerns related to a child or a new phase in life

The Mouse + The Fox

Honesty

The Mouse + The Bear

Uncertainties and insecurities turn into stability and firmness

The Mouse + The Star

Much thinking/pondering brings clarity

The Mouse + The Stork

Changes are happening

The Mouse + The Dog

Not showing much interest in friends

The Mouse + The Tower

Self-isolation

The Mouse + The Garden

Feeling uncomfortable in public

The Mouse + The Mountain

Overcoming hindrances and blockages

The Mouse + The Ways

Dealing with unpleasantness

The Mouse + The Heart

Uncomfortable situations in matters of the heart (love and relationships)

The Mouse + The Ring

No relationship (being single or divorced)

The Mouse + The Book

Secrets dissolve

The Mouse + The Letter

Delayed news

The Mouse + The Gentleman

Much thought about a man

The Mouse + The Lady

Much thought about a woman

The Mouse + The Lily

Prude ness (relationships without sexual involvements)

The Mouse + The Sun

Something is stealing the client's power and energy (examine surrounding cards)

The Mouse + The Moon

Confused emotions (not being able to think clearly)

The Mouse + The Key

Insecurity

The Mouse + The Fishes

Alcohol abuse (also, depression)

The Mouse + The Anchor

Unemployment (loss of job)

The Mouse + The Cross

Complete loss of something/someone

24 – The Heart
Jack of Hearts

General Meaning

The Heart speaks of love and happiness in all areas of the client's life. Everything is developing according to his or her hopes and dreams. Problems have been eliminated and the roads for happiness and success are wide open. The Heart usually indicates a period of great joy and a general feeling of being 'in love' and loved by others. Questioned about love and relationship, this card shows that the client has met his or her ideal partner and that the relationship is developing harmoniously. Work and employment develop smoothly and the client 'loves what he or she does'. However, should either The Tower (card 19) or The Mouse (card 23) be to the left or to the right of The Heart, then this can indicate that the client is cold-hearted and does not allow other people to come close to his or her heart.

Combinations

The Heart + The Cavalier

Activities related to matters of the heart

The Heart + The Clover

Luck in love

The Heart + The Ship

Positive developments in matters of love and relationships

The Heart + The House

Love for one's house and home (also, patriotism)

The Heart + The Tree

Lasting love

The Heart + The Clouds

Developments in matters of love and relationships create clarity

The Heart + The Snake

Love with hindrances

The Heart + The Coffin

No developments/stagnation in matters of love and relationships

The Heart + The Flowers

Visitors (good friends come to visit)

The Heart + The Scythe

Temperamental relationships

The Heart + The Whip

Discussions and strife with loved ones

The Heart + The Birds

Two loves/passions (not necessarily two partners)

The Heart + The Child

A new love/relationship

The Heart + The Fox

Dishonesty in matters of love and relationships

The Heart + The Bear

Jealousy and envy

The Heart + The Star

Fulfilled love (also, happiness)

The Heart + The Stork

Positive changes/developments in matters of love

The Heart + The Dog

A very good friendship

The Heart + The Tower

Boundaries in matters of love

The Heart + The Garden

A love for the outdoors

The Heart + The Mountain

Being unable to express emotions and feelings

The Heart + The Ways

Uncertain developments in matters of love

The Heart + The Mouse

Love sickness (also, loss of love/relationship)

The Heart + The Ring

A strong bond between lovers

The Heart + The Book

Secret love

The Heart + The Letter

Love letter/news from the client's partner

The Heart + The Gentleman

A charming man

The Heart + The Lady

A charming woman

The Heart + The Lily

Sexually fulfilled love

The Heart + The Sun

Being in love

The Heart + The Moon

Deep love

The Heart + The Key

Love with certainty

The Heart + The Fishes

Love of money

The Heart + The Anchor

Clinging to the partner/inseparable love

The Heart + The Cross

Problems in matters (related to past lives)

25 – The Ring
Ace of Clubs

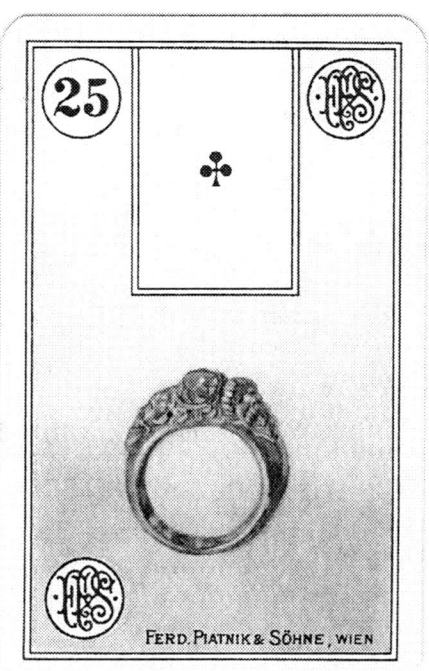

General Meaning

The true meaning of The Ring can only be interpreted in relation to its surrounding cards. It always speaks of relationships and partnership but also of duties and contracts. Questioned about love and relationships, The Ring speaks of happy and fulfilled marriages and stable relationships. In aspects of work and employment, it advises the client that his or her workplace is secure and stable.

Combinations

The Ring + The Cavalier

Proposing (for marriage)

The Ring + The Clover

Happy relationships/involvements

The Ring + The Ship

Relationships/involvements/love is coming

The Ring + The House

Stability at home (my home is my castle)

The Ring + The Tree

Stable relationships

The Ring + The Clouds

Uncertainties in matters of relationships leave

The Ring + The Snake

Relationships/involvements/love brings grieve and tears

The Ring + The Coffin

Divorce (also, being able to let go of past relationships)

The Ring + The Flowers

Relationships/involvements/love needs much work

The Ring + The Scythe

Dangerous relationships/involvements/love

The Ring + The Whip

Relationships/involvements/love brings strife and conflict

The Ring + The Birds

Two Relationships/involvements

The Ring + The Child

New Relationships/involvements

The Ring + The Fox

False developments in matters of relationships (against one's better judgment)

The Ring + The Bear

Long-term relationships/long marriage

The Ring + The Star

Success in Relationships/involvements/love

The Ring + The Stork

Unstable Relationships/involvements/love

The Ring + The Dog

Lasting friendships (not just a lover but also a friend)

The Ring + The Tower

Divorce (isolation from the partner)

The Ring + The Garden

Wedding

The Ring + The Mountain

Difficulties in relationships/involvements/love

The Ring + The Ways

Pursuing the same goals

The Ring + The Mouse

Loss of relationships/involvements/love

The Ring + The Heart

Deep love

The Ring + The Book

Pre-marital agreements

The Ring + The Letter

Superficial relationships/involvements/love

The Ring + The Gentleman

A married man (who is already in a relationship)

The Ring + The Lady

A married woman (who is already in a relationship)

The Ring + The Lily

Good relations to/with the family

The Ring + The Sun

Relationships/involvements/love bring security and stability

The Ring + The Moon

Soul mates

The Ring + The Key

Through thick and thin

The Ring + The Fishes

Being involved with money

The Ring + The Anchor

Unbreakable relationships/love

The Ring + The Cross

Relationships/involvements/love are meant to be

26 – The Book
Ten of Diamonds

General Meaning

The Book speaks of secrets and hidden information. Certain activities or plans should not be discussed yet. The client needs to learn to keep their secrets to him or herself as some people who are close to the client are not yet able or willing to hear what he or she has to say. Questioned about relationships, this card advises the client to keep his or her romantic involvements to themselves as this is not the time to discuss his or her relationship with others. If this is the last card to be dealt, then the client should be told that he or she will not be able to get the answers they came to find.

Combinations

The Book + The Cavalier

Sharing secrets (that still need to be kept secret)

The Book + The Clover

Keeping something secret for a short time

The Book + The Ship

A surprise journey (unexpected travels)

The Book + The House

A house with many secrets

The Book + The Tree

A secret that will never be revealed

The Book + The Clouds

Uncertainties and speculations will be cleared up

The Book + The Snake

A woman with many secrets

The Book + The Coffin

Feeling unwell (being sick for a short time)

The Book + The Flowers

A surprise

The Book + The Scythe

A secret will be revealed

The Book + The Whip

Secret talks/discussions

The Book + The Birds

A doubtful secret

The Book + The Child

A small secret

The Book + The Fox

The wrong documents/paperwork

The Book + The Bear

A secret is safe

The Book + The Star

Mysticism/secret knowledge related to supernatural matters

The Book + The Stork

Changes happen in secrecy

The Book + The Dog

A secret friendship

The Book + The Tower

Keeping a secret no matter what

The Book + The Garden

Secret organizations

The Book + The Mountain

Difficulties and blockages are not yet known

The Book + The Ways

A secret leads in different directions

The Book + The Mouse

Secret losses

The Book + The Heart

Secret love

The Book + The Ring

Secret relationships/involvements

The Book + The Letter

A secret letter (also, a letter containing very important and private information)

The Book + The Gentleman

An unknown person/a stranger

The Book + The Lady

An unknown person/a stranger

The Book + The Lily

A secret has revealed itself/will reveal itself

The Book + The Sun

Mysterious power and energy

The Book + The Moon

Secrets of the soul

The Book + The Key

The key to a secret

The Book + The Fishes

Secret money

The Book + The Anchor

A job involving books

The Book + The Cross

A secret from a past life

27 – The Letter
Seven of Spades

General Meaning

The Letter usually speaks of messages, letters, emails and all other types of correspondence. On a deeper level, this card also indicates something superficial, short-lived, without deeper meaning or far-reaching effects. In matters of love and relationship, The Letter speaks of personal messages from the client's partner. Questioned about work and employment, this card tells the client that he or she should not get side-tracked at work.

Combinations

The Letter + The Cavalier

A gift or present

The Letter + The Clover

A short message

The Letter + The Ship

News is on its way

The Letter + The House

News coming to the home of the client

The Letter + The Tree

Waiting for news

The Letter + The Clouds

News clears up uncertainties

The Letter + The Snake

News received indirectly

The Letter + The Coffin

News about medical examinations (such as diagnosis, test results)

The Letter + The Flowers

An invitation

The Letter + The Scythe

Sudden and unexpected news

The Letter + The Whip

News brings talks and discussions (far-reaching news)

The Letter + The Birds

Doubtful news

The Letter + The Child

A small present (a token of affection)

The Letter + The Fox

Wrong/false news (lies)

The Letter + The Bear

Official news (such as letters from a lawyer)

The Letter + The Star

Making contact (also, happy news)

The Letter + The Stork

News concerning positive developments/positive changes

The Letter + The Dog

Pen pal

The Letter + The Tower

Official news (such as letters from public/governmental office, the county/council)

The Letter + The Garden

Invitation to a large event

The Letter + The Mountain

Short delays

The Letter + The Ways

The quickest way

The Letter + The Mouse

News/message gets lost/got lost

The Letter + The Heart

Heart-felt news (also, love letter)

The Letter + The Ring

Invitation to attend a wedding

The Letter + The Book

News concerning a secret which is about to be revealed

The Letter + The Gentleman

Weak connections/relations concerning a man

The Letter + The Lady

Weak connections/relations concerning a woman

The Letter + The Lily

News about the family

The Letter + The Sun

News which brings strength and encouragement to the client

The Letter + The Moon

News which brings confidence to the client

The Letter + The Key

News will surely come

The Letter + The Fishes

A present (also a cheque or money order)

The Letter + The Anchor

A letter concerning work

The Letter + The Cross

Life-changing news

28 – The Gentleman
Ace of Hearts

General Meaning

More information on this card can be found in the section called *'Cards indicating Persons'* under *'Additional Combinations and Special Meanings'* from page 127 onwards.

Combinations

The Gentleman + The Cavalier

A very active/energetic gentleman

The Gentleman + The Clover

Only for a short while

The Gentleman + The Ship

He lives far away (long-distance relationship)

The Gentleman + The House

He is already there (the client knows the man already)

The Gentleman + The Tree

A partner for life

The Gentleman + The Clouds

A man with many secrets (also, mysterious, not very open)

The Gentleman + The Snake

A man with two woman

The Gentleman + The Coffin

No developments in terms of relationships (stagnation)

The Gentleman + The Flowers

Flirtation (a fling)

The Gentleman + The Scythe

Tensions

The Gentleman + The Whip

Strife and arguments

The Gentleman + The Birds

Uncertainty, not sure which choice to make

The Gentleman + The Child

A new beginning

The Gentleman + The Fox

A dishonest man

The Gentleman + The Bear

Decisions are influenced by the man's parents

The Gentleman + The Star

An intelligent and open gentleman

The Gentleman + The Stork

Relocation (moved home/is moving home)

The Gentleman + The Dog

A good friend

The Gentleman + The Tower

A stubborn man

The Gentleman + The Garden

Changing lifestyle, becoming less involved with society and parties

The Gentleman + The Mountain

He is blocking himself

The Gentleman + Ways

Laziness (also, not being determined but looking for easy alternatives)

The Gentleman + The Mouse

News concerning a woman

The Gentleman + The Heart

A charming gentleman

The Gentleman + The Ring

A married man (a man in a serious/long-term relationship)

The Gentleman + The Book

He is not yet known (not yet in the client's life)

The Gentleman + The Letter

Weak relations/connections

The Gentleman + The Lady

Good relations/connections

The Gentleman + The Lily

Sexual encounters (only based on sex)

The Gentleman + The Sun

Strong attraction

The Gentleman + The Moon

A deep, emotional connection

The Gentleman + The Key

A man brings security

The Gentleman + The Fishes

He loves money too much

The Gentleman + The Anchor

A stable person

The Gentleman + The Cross

He is led/brought about by destiny

29 – The Lady
Ace of Spades

General Meaning

More information on this card can be found in the section called *'Cards indicating Persons'* under *'Additional Combinations and Special Meanings'* from page 127 onwards.

Combinations

The Lady + The Cavalier

Moving forward with a clear goal in mind

The Lady + The Clover

Only for a short while

The Lady + The Ship

Going traveling

The Lady + The House

Separating from house and home

The Lady + The Tree

A partner for life

The Lady + The Clouds

Leaving uncertainties behind

The Lady + The Snake

A female friend (always older)

The Lady + The Coffin

Moving away from stagnation (finding new energy)

The Lady + The Flowers

A close female friend (always younger)

The Lady + The Scythe

Tensions

The Lady + The Whip

Moving away from strife and arguments

The Lady + The Birds

Uncertainties, not knowing what to do next

The Lady + The Child

A woman with a child (this child is very close to the woman and needs lots of attention)

The Lady + The Fox

An open and honest woman

The Lady + The Bear

Decisions are influenced by the woman's parents

The Lady + The Star

An intelligent and open woman

The Lady + The Stork

Relocation (moved/moving home or traveling)

The Lady + The Dog

A close, male friend

The Lady + The Tower

Looking for solitude, a desire to be alone

The Lady + The Garden

Looking for company, enjoys going out

The Lady + The Mountain

She is blocking herself due to stubbornness

The Lady + The Ways

Looking for alternatives

The Lady + The Mouse

Thinking/pondering over a man

The Lady + The Heart

A charming and friendly woman

The Lady + The Ring

A married woman (in a serious/long-term relationship)

The Lady + The Book

She is not yet known (not yet in the client's life)

The Lady + The Letter

Weak relations/connections

The Lady + The Gentleman

Tensions between partners

The Lady + The Lily

Sexual encounters (only based on sex)

The Lady + The Sun

Strong attraction

The Lady + The Moon

A deep, emotional connection

The Lady + The Key

A woman brings security

The Lady + The Fishes

A wealthy partner

The Lady + The Anchor

A stable woman

The Lady + The Cross

She is led/brought about by destiny

30 – The Lily
King of Spades

General Meaning

The Lily card speaks of harmony, sexuality, family, friends and balance but also of rest and stagnation in the client's life. Questioned about love and romance, this card shows that the client's relationships are stable and sexually fulfilling. If the client is single, then this is however not the time to pursue new romantic endeavors. The client's work and employment situation is also stable and he or she enjoys a 'familiar atmosphere' at their workplace. However, if the client is trying to see projects and activities come to fruition, then he or she should invest extra time and energy as these areas might feel 'stuck' and could suffer from stagnation.

Combinations

The Lily + The Cavalier

News about the family

The Lily + The Clover

Happy family

The Lily + The Ship

Traveling with family

The Lily + The House

The home/house of the family

The Lily + The Tree

This is not the time to find out

The Lily + The Clouds

Family tensions disappear

The Lily + The Snake

A female member of the family

The Lily + The Coffin

Sexual problems (can also indicate sexually transmitted diseases or diseases of the reproductive organs)

The Lily + The Flowers

Happy family (can also indicate cysts in the female client's womb/ovaries)

The Lily + The Scythe

News and ideas

The Lily + The Whip

Discussions/strife within the family

The Lily + The Birds

Having two sexual partners

The Lily + The Child

A new addition to the family

The Lily + The Fox

Not getting on with the family (also, not accepting one's sexuality)

The Lily + The Bear

The head of the family

The Lily + The Star

Drugs (either drug abuse or being on medication)

The Lily + The Stork

Changes within the family

The Lily + The Dog

Good friends that are members of the family

The Lily + The Tower

Not being able to have as much sex as the client wants

The Lily + The Garden

A brothel

The Lily + The Mountain

Having difficulties with the family

The Lily + The Ways

Decisions need to be made

The Lily + The Mouse

Having no sexual activities

The Lily + The Heart

Family comes to visit

The Lily + The Ring

An affair

The Lily + The Book

An affair needs to be kept secret

The Lily + The Letter

Irregular contact with the family

The Lily + The Gentleman

A sexual partner

The Lily + The Lady

A sexual partner

The Lily + The Sun

Finding comfort within the family

The Lily + The Moon

A harmonious phase

The Lily + The Key

Peace, love and fulfillment

The Lily + The Fishes

Financial backup from the family

The Lily + The Anchor

Serving the community

The Lily + The Cross

Helping each other out/supporting each other (in relation to family)

31 – The Sun
Ace of Diamonds

General Meaning

The Sun card brings strength, power, warmth, creativity and energy to the reading. It tells the client that he or she can expect his or her projects, hopes and wishes to come true. No blocks and hindrances can keep the client from reaching his or her goals. Questioned especially about love and romance, this card tells the client that he or she can expect luck and happiness in his or her existing relationships. Should the client be single, then new romantic endeavors are on the horizon. Unexpected possibilities will also open up at the client's work place. Speaking about health and wellbeing, The Sun tells the client that he or she can expect to feel better and fully recover soon. However, this card also advises the client to take good care of his or her eyes at this time.

Combinations

The Sun + The Cavalier

Moving on to something better

The Sun + The Clover

Energy and strength bring happiness and success

The Sun + The Ship

Energy and strength bring positive movements

The Sun + The House

Comfort and security at home

The Sun + The Tree

Finding lasting energy and strength

The Sun + The Clouds

Positive developments

The Sun + The Snake

Having difficulties to find security

The Sun + The Coffin

No one can stop you

The Sun + The Flowers

It is time to act now

The Sun + The Scythe

The client has so much energy that they do not know what to do with it (a desire to do something, anything!)

The Sun + The Whip

Very energetic/energized discussions

The Sun + The Birds

Insecurity and uncertainty make way for new energy and strength

The Sun + The Child

Finding new sources of energy and strength

The Sun + The Fox

Things are not what they seem to be

The Sun + The Bear

Stability

The Sun + The Star

Complete success (this card combination also talks about diplomats and politicians)

The Sun + The Stork

Comfort and security create positive changes

The Sun + The Dog

A good and supportive friend

The Sun + The Tower

Using power and strength resourcefully

The Sun + The Garden

Exciting events/parties

The Sun + The Mountain

Energy and strength is blocked

The Sun + The Ways

Moving forward with determination and strength

The Sun + The Mouse

Feeling drained

The Sun + The Heart

Being in love

The Sun + The Ring

Comfort and security in relationships

The Sun + The Book

Comfort and security will soon show

The Sun + The Letter

Positive news

The Sun + The Gentleman

Attraction

The Sun + The Lady

Attraction

The Sun + The Lily

Comfort and security within the family

The Sun + The Moon

Receiving something (could be a present, a message, a gift)

The Sun + The Key

Strength and energy are present

The Sun + The Fishes

Financial success

The Sun + The Anchor

A strong connection to work/employment (finding fulfillment in one's job)

The Sun + The Cross

Positive endings

More information on **The Sun** can be found on page 139.

32 – The Moon
Eight of Hearts

General Meaning

The Moon symbolizes the client's feelings, sensitivity and emotional needs. Questioned on its own, this card shows that the client has sentimental tendencies and suffers from moodiness. It advises the client to rest and not to overly engage in social activities. Speaking about matters of the heart, this card shows that the client's relationships are characterized by deep emotions and closeness. He or she has also put their heart and soul into their job and actively engage in many of the projects at the work place. When asked about health and wellbeing, this card warns the client of depression and mental illnesses.

Combinations

The Moon + The Cavalier

Recognition and success for the client

The Moon + The Clover

A little recognition

The Moon + The Ship

Alcohol (-ism)

The Moon + The House

Emotional ups and downs at home

The Moon + The Tree

Unshakable stability

The Moon + The Clouds

Emotional uncertainties leave

The Moon + The Snake

Recognition is coming with delays

The Moon + The Coffin

Heavy depression

The Moon + The Flowers

Spiritual/emotional growth

The Moon + The Scythe

Sudden emotional upheavals

The Moon + The Whip

Listening to too many voices/opinions

The Moon + The Birds

Being out of balance

The Moon + The Child

Mediumistic abilities/experiences

The Moon + The Fox

Self-deception

The Moon + The Bear

Emotional stability

The Moon + The Star

Seeing things for what they truly are

The Moon + The Stork

Change of personality/change in behavior

The Moon + The Dog

Finding recognition amongst friends

The Moon + The Tower

Mental health institution

The Moon + The Garden

Receiving recognition from others

The Moon + The Mountain

Emotional blocks

The Moon + The Ways

Finding recognition by following alternative courses of action

The Moon + The Mouse

Depressive tendencies

The Moon + The Heart

Harmony

The Moon + The Ring

Harmonious relationships

The Moon + The Book

Not being aware of received recognition and appreciation

The Moon + The Letter

Connection with others on an emotional level

The Moon + The Gentleman

Deep emotional connection to one's partner/spouse

The Moon + The Lady

Deep emotional connection to one's partner/spouse

The Moon + The Lily

Deep emotional connection to one's family

The Moon + The Sun

Being open to hear the voice of spirit (clairvoyance)

The Moon + The Key

Good mediumistic development

The Moon + The Fishes

Financial success

The Moon + The Anchor

Recognition and success related to work

The Moon + The Cross

Unconsciously

More information on **The Moon** can be found on page 137.

33 – The Key
Eight of Diamonds

General Meaning

Whereas The Book (card 26) speaks of secrets and hidden information that are not yet or can not yet be revealed, The Key indicates that some secrets are about to come to the light. If every card in the Lenormand Deck would be given one word, this card would simply be called 'yes'. It is important to note that the card after or to the left of The Key always indicates what is surely coming or manifesting. Questioned on its own, this card tells the client that his or her plans will come true with 100% security. Relationships as well as work and employment are secure and stable.

Combinations

The Key + The Cavalier

Always happy and friendly

The Key + The Clover

Always quick, swift and short-lived

The Key + The Ship

Movement and positive development will definitely come

The Key + The House

It is meant to happen

The Key + The Tree

Success in life

The Key + The Clouds

Uncertainties and doubts definitely disappear

The Key + The Snake

Delays and detours in life/projects are definitely over

The Key + The Coffin

Sickness is coming

The Key + The Flowers

A pleasant surprise

The Key + The Scythe

Tensions and strife is definitely leaving

The Key + The Whip

Talks and discussions will definitely happen

The Key + The Birds

Doubts about which course of action to choose

The Key + The Child

News is definitely coming

The Key + The Fox

Caution is definitely needed

The Key + The Bear

Stability is definitely coming/present

The Key + The Star

Mediumistic abilities and clairvoyance is definitely present

The Key + The Stork

Changes will definitely happen!

The Key + The Dog

Definitely a trustworthy friend

The Key + The Tower

Boundaries can not be overcome

The Key + The Garden

The event/party/meeting will definitely happen

The Key + The Mountain

Something is definitely blocking the progress

The Key + The Ways

A decision will definitely be made

The Key + The Mouse

Something is/will definitely be lost

The Key + The Heart

Love is definitely stable

The Key + The Ring

Relationship/marriage is definitely stable

The Key + The Book

Secret plans will come to fruition

The Key + The Letter

News is definitely coming

The Key + The Gentleman

A man that can be trusted

The Key + The Lady

A woman that can be trusted

The Key + the Lily

Sexual desires will definitely be fulfilled

The Key + The Sun

Comfort and security will definitely be found

The Key + The Moon

Mediumistic abilities are definitely present

The Key + The Fishes

Financial success is definitely coming

The Key + The Anchor

Success and recognition at work is definitely coming

The Key + The Cross

This is definitely a matter of destiny (it is definitely meant to happen)

34 – The Fishes
King of Diamonds

General Meaning

The Fishes speaks about the client's finances and material belongings. It also warns the client to face his or her problems more readily as the client has a tendency to 'sit and wait' – and sometimes for to long! Especially the client's finances, which need more attention at this time. Questioned about matters of the heart, this card promises security. In matters of work and employment, The Fishes speaks of higher incomes, pay raises and changes which will bring higher earnings. However, this card also warns the client not to indulge in alcoholic beverages to much. The client's Kidneys, Liver, Bladder and his or her emotional state need special attention at this time also.

Combinations

The Fishes + The Cavalier
Money is coming

The Fishes + The Clover
Short-lived/quick money which will not last

The Fishes + The Ship
Money is 'flowing in'

The Fishes + The House
Money is coming to the house/home

The Fishes + The Tree

Finances are stabilizing

The Fishes + The Clouds

Uncertainties in financial matters (also, negative or unpleasant financial situations)

The Fishes + The Snake

Uncertainties in financial matters come to an end

The Fishes + The Coffin

Assets with dead capital (such as property/stocks/bonds)

The Fishes + The Flowers

Emotional involvements

The Fishes + The Scythe

Sudden/unexpected money

The Fishes + The Whip

Discussions/talks/negotiations related to financial matters

The Fishes + The Birds

Money from two sources (also, investments double)

The Fishes + The Child

A little bit of money

The Fishes + The Fox

Dishonesty in financial matters

The Fishes + The Bear

Stable finances

The Fishes + The Star

Plenty of money

The Fishes + The Stork

Financial improvement

The Fishes + The Dog

Connection on an emotional level

The Fishes + The Tower

Tax Office, IRS (UK: Inland Revenue)

The Fishes + The Garden

Gambling for/with money

The Fishes + The Mountain

Kidney stones

The Fishes + The Ways

Giving too much money away

The Fishes + The Mouse

Losing money

The Fishes + The Heart

Love 'with heart and soul'

The Fishes + The Ring

Financial involvements (also, marriage for money)

The Fishes + The Book

Secret money/investments

The Fishes + The Letter

Stocks/bonds

The Fishes + The Gentleman

A wealthy man

The Fishes + The Lady

A woman who loves money too much (also, a predictable woman)

The Fishes + The Lily

Money is coming to the family

The Fishes + The Sun

A lot of money is coming

The Fishes + The Moon

Financial recognition/bonuses

The Fishes + The Key

Building financial stability

The Fishes + The Anchor

Money is coming via self-employment (also, cash-in-hand employment, non-taxable money)

The Fishes + The Cross

Emotional strains are taken away

More information on **The Fishes** can be found on page 140.

35 – The Anchor
Nine of Spades

General Meaning

The Anchor usually speaks about the client's work and employment but can also mean school, university or other types of higher education. On a deeper level, this card also indicates addictions and obsessions. The general message of this card is to invest more time and energy at the workplace. Even though other areas of the client's life might temporarily suffer, the engagement he or she will bring to the workplace will shortly pay off and will lay an excellent foundation for the future. Questioned in matters of love, this card warns the client not to develop addictions or obsessions towards his or her partner.

Combinations

The Anchor + The Cavalier

Being 'on your legs' (a job that involves much walking around)

The Anchor + The Clover

Liking work only for a short while

The Anchor + The Ship

Traveling with/for work

The Anchor + The House

Working from home

The Anchor + The Tree

A job for life

The Anchor + The Clouds

Further education, studies

The Anchor + The Snake

Faking it at work (being successful because of sneakiness)

The Anchor + The Coffin

Not feeling comfortable at work

The Anchor + The Flowers

Using much creativity at work

The Anchor + The Scythe

Working with metals

The Anchor + The Whip

A job that involves much talking and communicating

The Anchor + The Birds

Having two jobs (can also indicate working for the Police Force)

The Anchor + The Child

Working with children

The Anchor + The Fox

The wrong job (can also indicate working for the Secret Service, detective work)

The Anchor + The Bear

Management position

The Anchor + The Star

Working in the medical field (or Pharmacology)

The Anchor + The Stork

Change of employment

The Anchor + The Dog

Working in the service industry

The Anchor + The Tower

Teacher, Civil Servant (working for the government)

The Anchor + The Garden

Working with many people (in a large company or dealing with the public)

The Anchor + The Mountain

Working with stones (Builders, Architects)

The Anchor + The Ways

Versatility

The Anchor + The Mouse

Recycling

The Anchor + The Heart

Much love for the job

The Anchor + The Ring

Being 'married to the job'

The Anchor + The Book

Working with books

The Anchor + The Letter

Office jobs

The Anchor + The Gentleman

A conservative man

The Anchor + The Lady

A conservative woman

The Anchor + The Lily

Working with/for the family

The Anchor + The Sun

Finding fulfillment through/in one's job

The Anchor + The Moon

Being emotionally attached to the job

The Anchor + The Key

Working with keys (security service, security guard)

The Anchor + The Fishes

Working with money (banking)

The Anchor + The Cross

Spiritual vocation

36 – The Cross
Six of Clubs

General Meaning

The Cross speaks of burdens, endings and swift changes. The card before or to the left of The Cross shows influences, persons or situations who's power in the client's life is decreasing or waning. The card after or to the right of The Cross shows influences, persons or situations who's power in the client's life is increasing and become more and more dominant and popular. Cards underneath or below The Cross usually indicate influences, persons or situations that are linked to the client's destiny. Questioned about matters of the heart, this card tells the client that his or her relationships are about to be shaken and tested. Speaking about work and employment, this card indicates burdens and extra hours at the client's workplace.

Combinations

The Cross + The Cavalier
Plans and projects are burdens

The Cross + The Clover
Short-lived burdens (stress will not last long)

The Cross + The Ship
An eventful journey

The Cross + The House
Troubles at the house/home (a feeling of heaviness)

The Cross + The Tree

Not an easy life

The Cross + The Clouds

Karmic worries (can not be easily ignored)

The Cross + The Snake

Grief and sorrows

The Cross + The Coffin

Life-lessons will be learned

The Cross + The Flowers

Pleasantness comes to an end

The Cross + The Scythe

Not fulfilling one's destiny (trying to avoid it)

The Cross + The Whip

Far-reaching talks and discussions

The Cross + The Birds

Finally making decisions

The Cross + The Child

A hard/difficult childhood

The Cross + The Fox

Falsehood

The Cross + The Bear

Making necessary compromises

The Cross + The Star

The client's destiny (closely examine surrounding cards)

The Cross + The Stork

Karmic involvements

The Cross + The Dog

Karmic friendship (friendship that is meant to be)

The Cross + The Tower

Hospital

The Cross + The Garden

The cemetery

The Cross + The Mountain

It is not meant to be!

The Cross + The Ways

It will happen within the next 7 weeks

The Cross + The Mouse

Complete loss of someone or something

The Cross + The Heart

Karmic love (it is meant to be)

The Cross + The Ring

Relationship comes to an end (divorce)

The Cross + The Book

An important secret with far-reaching effects

The Cross + The Letter

A letter with far-reaching effects

The Cross + The Gentleman

The destined partner (this is meant to be)

The Cross + The Lady

The destined partner (this is meant to be)

The Cross + The Lily

A very close-knit family

The Cross + The Sun

Strength and energy

The Cross + The Moon

Intuition

The Cross + The Key

It is meant to happen

The Cross + The Fishes

Soul-mates from previous lives

The Cross + The Anchor

The destined job

More information on **The Cross** can be found on page 140

ADDITIONAL COMBINATIONS AND SPECIAL MEANINGS

Cards indicating Persons

The Lady and **The Gentleman** are the two most obvious Person Cards in the deck. You should begin your reading by examining where these two cards are in the Great Spread. Some newer Lenormand decks have changed the direction into which either The Gentleman and/or The Lady 'look', and designed the cards in such as way, that both look in the same direction. This makes professional readings harder and can bring serious confusion. As, according to the old Lenormand cards, the direction into which the cards 'look' indicates what lies ahead of the client. This can be tricky to remember as The Gentleman card looks 'ahead' or in the direction in which the cards are laid out. The Lady looks backwards so to speak!

From my personal experiences and from information obtained from other readers, I can say that 90% of all clients have questions regarding relationships, love and romance. All cards in between The Gentleman and The Lady indicate what 'lies between' the couple. This can be read diagonal as well as vertically. If the Lady and The Gentleman 'look' at each other or 'face' each other, then the couple is very harmonious. If the cards lie 'with their backs to each other' then the couple doesn't have much to say to each other. The card which appears first whilst the cards are laid out is most likely the more dominant partner in the relationship.

Hint: Don't just look which card comes first to see if the cards face each other or if the cards face away from each other! Draw an imaginary line between the two cards, and see if they face each other or if the look away from each other 'along this line'.

The Lady

If your client is female, then use this card as the Person Card - The Lady represents your female client in all cases. If your client is male, then this card always speaks about his 'Lady of the heart'. If your client is a married man but 'otherwise involved', then this card can be interpreted as the client's love affair - his wife would be represented as **The Snake**.

The Gentleman

If your client is male, then use this card as Person Card - The Gentleman represents your male client in all cases. If your client is female, then this card always speaks about the 'man of her heart'. If your client is a married woman but 'otherwise involved', then this card can be interpreted as the client's love affair – her husband would be represented as **The Bear**.

In addition to their 'usual' meaning, the following cards can be also read as person cards:

The Cavalier

A nice, pleasant and charming young man

The Snake

An intelligent Woman

The Flowers

A nice, pleasant and charming woman

The Birds

Either a couple or two older woman

The Child

The client's own children, or a child/teenager.

The Fox

A sly and tricky person

The Bear

A nice and helpful older man, a father figure or a male superior

The Dog

A good and faithful friend - either male or female

The Tower

An egotistical man; an unpleasant superior

The Mountain

A dominant and frustrated man or superior

Cards indicating Times and Time Frames

The following cards can be read as Time Frames as well as their 'usual' meaning:

The Flowers

Spring

The Clover

3-4 days

The Tree

9-12 months, also 'the afternoon' and autumn.

The Star

In the evening, during the night (also, winter)

The Sun

In the morning, before noon. Also summer.

The Ways

7 Weeks

The Letter

Only for a short time, or 'soon'

The Moon

In the evening

The Cross

2-3 weeks

The Lily

Winter

Concerning Relationships

In the Great Spread, find **The Lady** and **The Gentleman** in the cards. All cards BETWEEN these two, give clues to relationships. Also find The Ring and examine that card's surroundings to find more information on the romantic relationships of your client. The following card combinations also indicate relationships and interpersonal affairs.

The Ring

Relationship

The Flowers + The Ring

Engagement

The Ring + The Letter + The Cavalier

A marriage proposal

The Ring + The Birds OR **The Ring + The Whip**

Two (possible) relationships

The Heart + The Whip + The Birds

Two affairs

The Heart + The Whip OR **The Birds + The Lily**

Two passionate affairs, which might cause difficulties within the client's family life

The Clouds + The Ring

Can indicate a divorce or the death of the client's partner, this should, however, be investigated further before any statements related to the end of the client's relationships are made!

Concerning Work and Employment

Look for **The Anchor** and again examine all surrounding cards. Should you find Person cards, then this most likely indicates colleagues, co-workers and/or superiors - especially if The Bear (card 15) is near The Anchor (card 35).

The Anchor + The Cavalier + The House

Stables, Fitness centers, gyms

The Anchor + The Cavalier + The Clover

Cabs, Taxis and similar forms of transport

The Anchor + The Clover

Temp work, Contracting

The Anchor + The Ship

Travel and Leisure Industry

The Anchor + The House + The Garden

Large company, working with the public

The Anchor + The Garden + The Flowers

Public relations or other occupation's which involves contact with the public

The Anchor + The Tower

Self-employed, independent work

The House + The Cavalier + The Ship

Tourist Guide, Flight attendant, Cabin crew

The House + The Cavalier + The Lily + The Garden + The Fishes + The Heart

Prostitution, Escort Services

The House + The Tree

A job for life

The House + The Clouds

Further education

The House + The Clouds above **The Anchor**

Chemical industry, gas works

The House + The Coffin

Can indicate jobs such as funeral director, undertaker or graveyard caretaker. It can also indicate illegal employment and 'cash in hand' jobs. It can also show that the client is not happy at his job due to difficulties with colleagues.

The House + The Flowers

Work involving artistic talents. This combination also shows that the client enjoys his job!

The House + The Flowers

Alternative healthcare

The House + The Flowers + The Coffin

Jobs in the care industry, such as nursing

The House + The Scythe + The Fishes

Jobs involving computers. This can range from office clerk to work in the IT sector

The House + The Scythe + The House

Dangerous work

The House + The Scythe

All work involving metal and iron, such a mechanic or work in the construction industry

The House + The Scythe + The Cavalier as well as **The Cavalier + The House + The Scythe**

Bailiff and similar jobs involving the collection of money

The House + The Whip

Jobs involving communication, translation or interpretation

The House + The Whip + The Letter

Secretarial jobs, Personal Assistant

The House + The Birds

Social work, Police

The House + The Birds + The Coffin

Work in a retirement home or generally working with the elderly

The House + The Child

This can either indicate jobs involving children or a new job

The House + The Fox

The wrong job

The House + The Fox + The Book + The Scythe

Government agencies, mainly the collection of information and statistics

The House + The Book + The Fox

Private detective

Concerning Friendships

Find **The Dog, The Flowers, The Snake** and **The Bear**. All these cards can give information on the client's circle of friends.

Concerning Financial Matters

Look for **The Fishes** and its surrounding cards.

The Fishes + The Whip

Financial talks

The Fishes + The Mouse

Indicates that the client is losing money

The Fishes + The Letter

Cheques and other financial transactions related to banks

The Fishes + The Child

A small amount of money

The Birds + The Fishes

Money received from two different sources, investments might double in value

The Anchor + The Fishes

Indicates stable finances

The Clouds + The Fishes

A temporary loss of money

The Snake + The Fishes

Indicates that money is coming, but it will be delayed and from unexpected sources

The Cavalier + The Fishes

Money is coming as a positive surprise

The Whip + The Fishes

Discussions and arguments over money

The Fox + The Fishes

The client is not handling his or her money very well

The Scythe + The Fishes

Loss of money

The Coffin + The Fishes

'Lost' money – or money that the client considers as lost – is returned

The Star + The Fishes

An amount of more then 1.000,-

The Clover + The Fishes

Money will be available but will not last

The Fishes + The Star + The Sun

Speak about an amount of more then 10.000,-

The Mountain + The Fishes

Indicate that the client needs to watch and save his money

The Mountain + The Clouds + The Fishes

A shortage of private funds

The Mountain + The Garden + The Fishes

Overall financial difficulties

The Clouds + The Anchor + The Fishes

Financial difficulties related to business ventures

The Tower + The Mountain + The Fishes + The Lady

A frugal woman

The Tower + The Mountain + The Fishes + The Gentleman

A frugal man

The Fishes + The Star + The Moon + The Sun

Speak about an amount of more then 100.000,-

The Fishes + The Star + The Moon + The Sun + The Tower

Speak about an amount of more then 500.000,-

The Ship + The Cross + The Fishes

Inheritances

Concerning Heath

Look for **The Coffin** as well as **The Tree**. Try and be careful with health predictions though! It is not advisable to tell people that they are going to die from a heart attack or lung cancer. It would be better to tell your clients to 'go for a check-up' and take better care of their health. The end of an illness (**The Coffin + The Mouse**) or excellent health (**The Tree + The Sun**) can and should be told whenever these combinations arise. Also bear in mind the following combinations, which can give some more clues on specific areas.

The Cavalier + The Scythe

Problems in the lower legs, most likely related to the sinews

The Cavalier + The Bear

'Heavy legs' and problems walking

The Cavalier + The Sun

Sweating

The Ship
Points towards the client's bladder but also to the soul!
The Ship + The Coffin

Sea- and travel-sickness, vomiting and fainting

The Ship + The Mountain + The Star

Diabetes

The Whip + The Fishes

Kidney problems (the left kidney is to weak)

The House speaks about the whole body.

The House + The Bear

Obesity

The House + The Mouse

Indicates diseases which have not yet manifested

The House + The Fishes

Points towards the Gall Bladder

The House + The Fishes + The Whip + The Cross

Diseases of the Gall Bladder related to stress, grief and anger

The House + The Clouds + The Cross

Diseases of the immune system, weakness of the body and pale skin

The House + The Mountain + The Clouds + The Cross

A slowly progressing disease. In the same instance, it can also indicate a slow healing process.

The House + The Tower + The Scythe + The Coffin + The Cross

A quick and painless death

The Tree stands for general health and wellbeing.

The Tree + The Clouds

Quick recovery from diseases

The Clouds + The Tree

A sudden illness

The Tree + The Coffin

Ill health is rooted in mental imbalances. Some readers would say that the client's illnesses and diseases are 'only in the mind'

The Tree + The Flowers
Cysts, growths
The Tree + The Birds

Fainting and mental 'ups and downs'

The Tree + The Moon

Depressive tendencies

The Tree + The Sun

Stable health

The Tree + The Sun + The Child

Pregnancy and easy birth

The Tree + The Fishes + The Ship

Too much water in the body

The Tree + The Stork + The Child

Pregnancy

The Tree + The Stork + The Scythe

A heavy and somewhat problematic pregnancy, possibly Caesarian Section

The Tree + The Stork + The Fox

Miscarriage

The Tree + The Stork + The Mouse

Indicates infertility

The Clouds card is associates with the respiratory system, the lungs and the chest. It also indicates that the client is prone to occasional, minor illnesses.

The Clouds + The Fox

Diseases of the throat, such as tonsillitis and loss of voice

The Clouds + The Mouse

Speaks of serious illnesses

The Clouds + The Coffin

Prolonged sickness

The Clouds + The Coffin + The Cavalier

A broken or swollen ankle

The Clouds + The Coffin + The Whip

A broken or swollen wrist

The Clouds + The Scythe + The Whip

These cards warn the client to be more careful, as he or she is in danger of accidents

The Clouds + The Coffin + The Cross

Indicates a fatality

The Clouds + The Child + The Scythe

Termination of pregnancy – either willingly or by accident

The Clouds + The Stork + The Scythe

Abortion

The Clouds + The Lily + The Coffin

Problems of the lower abdomen

The Clouds + The Lily + The Scythe

Diseases of the female reproductive organs

The Clouds + The Moon

Depression (Lunacy)

The Clouds + The Moon + The Coffin

Indicates that depression is caused by spirit influences

The Clouds + The Cross + The Scythe

Can point towards cancer

The Clouds + The Cross + The Fox

Can indicate that the client is NOT in danger of cancer at this time and that, if the client is either worried or has been given a diagnosis, the client needs to see another physician

Concerning Domestic Life

Look for **The House** and its surrounding cards.

Children

Examine the surrounding of **The Child**. If the client has no children, then this card can also indicate other heirs.

Parents

Cards in between **The Bear** and **The Tower** give information on the father of the client. Cards in between **The Snake** and **The Tower** speak about the client's mother.

Hint: Should you find **The Bear** or **The Snake** in one corner of The Great Spread and **The Tower** in another, then this indicates that the client's life is still very much influenced by his or her parents. The Bear in one corner and The Tower in another would indicate a strong influence of the father, The Snake in one corner and The Tower in another indicates a strong link to the mother.

Mystical & Spiritual Meanings of the Cards

As if fortune telling is not mystical and metaphysical enough, some cards can also give specific clues to the client's destiny as well as the spiritual influences surrounding or influencing him or her. As a spiritual reader and adviser, it is our responsibility to point our clients towards a happy and fulfilled life. Within Umbanda and Quimbanda, a person's happiness, health and general wellbeing is always associated with the person's destiny or life-path. Contrary to some Eastern Philosophies, poverty, suffering and sickness are not seen as 'karmic depths', which have to be paid in this life to achieve enlightenment or a 'better reincarnation'. What matters most is 'right here, right now'. No person can change the parts of their life that have already gone, and the discovery of past lives is nothing we concern ourselves with too much.

Within Umbanda and Quimbanda, to have a happy and fulfilled life means to be 'in tune' with our destiny - with god's plan for our life. Health, wealth and happiness are what the universe has intended us to have while we are on this earth, and to point people towards the achievement of these goals means to help them fulfill their destiny. This should not be interpreted wrongly though! The hoarding of treasures and a ruthless chasing after riches and fame is as much 'out of tune' as a tendency towards suffering and denial. Each and every individual will measure happiness differently, but the general rule is that if something is missing, then divination can give clues and hints on how to re-establish a balance and fill the gaps. Cards such as **The Clouds, The Coffin, The Scythe, The Star, The Sun, The Moon, The Fishes** and **The Cross** can give us some special insight into this balance.

The Clouds

This card generally represents the spirit world. Should any one of the Card's indicating Persons (see page 127-128) be shown next to The Clouds, then this shows that a spirit of similar or identical characteristics represented in that particular person card is showing his or her presence. If a card indicating persons appears either before or to the left of The Clouds, then this shows that this particular spirit is still very much earth-bound. It is very possible that the person/spirit died a forceful and sudden death or was under the influence of drugs or alcohol at the moment of death. In either case, this spirit is in need of spiritual elevation. If the name of this spirit is known, then a white candle should be lit and the following prayer should be said in dedication to that spirit for a period of 7 days:

God of clemency and mercy,
May Your goodness extend to all the Spirits I recommend to You in my prayers,
especially the Spirit of ...
Good Spirits, whose occupation is to do good, intercede together with me for his/her relief.
Make a ray of hope shine before their eyes and enlighten them as to the imperfections,
which maintain them distant from the homes of the blessed.
Open their hearts to repentance and the desire to cleanse themselves,
so they may accelerate their advancement.
Make them understand it is by their own efforts that they may shorten
the duration of their trials.
May God, in all His goodness, give them the necessary strength
to persevere with their good resolutions!
May these words, infused with benevolence, soften their trials, showing them
that there are on Earth those who sympathize and wish them happiness.

It is best to either light a white 7-Day candle and move it up a level each day by putting books under it, or to light a fresh candle every day and to move the candle holder higher each day in the same way. A card indicating persons either after or to the right of The Clouds shows that a confused and stray spirit is close to the client. In this case, the card before or to the left of The Clouds can give more information of this spirit and situation. It is best to advise the client to either have a series of Cleansing Baths (see Part III) or to seek help from a spiritual worker to remove the influence of this spirit.

The Coffin

This card can give information on previous incarnations. It is important to note the concept of reincarnation is not the same as in many of the Eastern and Hindu Religions. Contrary to some Eastern Philosophies, poverty, suffering and sickness are not seen as 'karmic depths', which have to be paid in this life to achieve enlightenment or a 'better reincarnation'. What matters most is 'right here, right now'. No person can change the parts of their life that have already gone, and the discovery of past lives is nothing we concern ourselves with to much. However, the experiences, sufferings and happiness we experience in past lives definitely influence's our decisions and characteristics in this life. If for example we found happiness in a particular spiritual path, past-time, area of employment or in a foreign country, then our incarnated spirit will drive our search for fulfillment in this life until we are able to again find what once brought us joy and happiness. It is my strong belief that the industrial revolution, the spread of religion and also the boom of the travel industry is driven by search for fulfillment of many people's incarnated spirits. The Coffin can also give information on a person's death in a previous incarnation. **The Scythe** to the left of The Coffin for example indicates that the person died a forceful death. The next card to the left of the Scythe would then show the injured or afflicted body part. If The Coffin appears in questions on love and relationships, then this can show that two people were already linked in a previous incarnation, but were separated by death. **The Coffin + The Star** can indicate that the client is having disturbing dreams as well as restless or sleepless nights. The client's 'sixth sense' is blurred and he or she is not as alert as usual. This combination can indicate that the client is in danger and further investigations should be done to find the source of these influences, and to determine what can be done to help the client. A combination of **The Cloud + The Sun + The Coffin** for example usually shows that some other form of witchcraft has been used to influence the client. There have been no spirit entities invoked to cause harm, but someone has used other means to influence the client. Further investigations should be done to find the source of these influences, and to determine what can be done to help the client.

The Scythe

This card is traditionally seen as the card of witchcraft. Different people have different opinions on what witchcraft is, and many doubt that something so superstitious and outdated actually exists. This section of the book was not added to convince anyone of the existence of witchcraft. It is intended to give those, who believe in the reality of supernatural forces, or even practice witchcraft to some extent, some clues, on how its influence can be 'detected' by means of this unique divination deck. As a simple definition, witchcraft can be any supernatural influence trying to manipulate your client, brought about by another person. This can range from an actual spell or working which has been directed to influence the client, to the unconscious use of supernatural forces towards the client by another individual. The most obvious indicator of Witchcraft is **The**

Moon + The Scythe. Some readers speak of 'black magic' whenever this combination appears in the spread. Within Umbanda and Quimbanda circles, this combination shows that someone is invoking the aid of Exu or Pomba Gira* to harm the client. This can also mean that some other form of witchcraft has been used against the client, but it always indicates the involvement of spirit entities. Further investigations should be done to find the source of these influences, and to determine what can be done to help the client.

The Star

This card generally speaks about spirits and spirit influences, as well as mediumistic abilities. Should **The Star + The Sun + The Gentleman** or **The Star + The Sun + The Lady** appear in a reading, then this shows that the client has strong mediumistic abilities. If The Star appears next to **The Coffin**, then this shows that he client has the ability to 'Dream True' – he or she can see future happenings in dreams. **The Clover** followed by The Star shows the client's ability to Astral Travel. Combinations of **The Star + The Bear** speak about the client's spirit guides or 'Guardian Angel'. Depending how close this combination appears to the Person Card shows how well attuned the client is to his or her Guardian Spirit.

The Sun

The client's destiny and special abilities can be identified in the cards close to The Sun. If this card appears to the left of the Person Card, then this shows us that the client is spiritually well attuned and able to incorporate his or her spirituality very well into his or her daily life. It also shows that the client is a very energetic person, full of energy and able to live life to its fullest. He or she is not only spiritually gifted but can also be very successful in their career and all other projects he or she undertakes. If we find a combination of **The Sun + The Whip + Person Card** or **Person Card + The Whip + The Sun** then this shows that the client is a natural Spiritual Healer.

The Moon

Psychic and spiritual abilities as well as the client's spiritual make-up can be seen in the cards surrounding The Moon. If this card appears to the left of the Person Card, then this shows us that we are dealing with a very spiritual person. This client has strong mediumistic abilities and deep intuition. He or she is very well attuned with his or her 'Higher Self' and can easily understand complex spiritual matters. This client has lived through many incarnations, was able to 'live and breath' many different spiritual traditions and mysteries and is in this incarnation able to 'connect the dots'. A combination of **The Clouds + The Moon + The Coffin** however indicates that depression is caused by spirit influences. It should be determined if this depression is caused either by the client's ancestors or if it is due to spirit influences which were sent to distract the client. No matter the outcome of the investigation, a cleansing ceremony should be performed and the 'spirits in questions' should be dealt with – either be placated or dispatched.

---

*For further information on Quimbanda see *Na Gira do Exu* by Mario dos Ventos, Lulu publishing, 2006.

The Fishes

This card speaks about the client's soul. If this card appears either to the left or to the right of the Person Card, then we know that this client is deeply emotional and can change his or her moods very quickly. However, we will always have to examine the card on the other side of The Fishes to get a clear picture of the state of the client's soul. A devastating experience such as the loss of a loved one or job might affect the client only for a short while. He or she can emotionally be 'on top of the world' one day and deeply devastated the next. In the light of previous incarnations we might tell the client that he or she was not able or allowed to show his or her emotions freely. The client's spirit has now chosen this present lifetime to give his or her emotions 'free rule'. When this card appears next to the Person Card, then the client should also be told to follow and live his or her dreams.

The Cross

Information on the client's destiny can be obtained from the cards surrounding The Cross. If this card appears to the left of the Person Card, then the card to the left of The Cross can give insight into the burdens and difficulties that the client is encountering - either at the present moment or around the time and situation which is questioned when using the cards. If we find **The Scythe + The Coffin + The Cross + The Person Card**, then this shows a violent death caused by the person's beliefs and ideology in a past life. If we find The Ring at the end of this combination, then this shows that the client is again in danger of losing his or her life due to religious fundamentalism.

Summery of Mystical and Spiritual Card-Combinations

The Cavalier + The Star

Astral Travel

The Clouds + The Sun

Negative influences

The Clouds + The Sun + The Coffin

Black Magic

The Clouds + The Moon

Negative influences from spirit guide (1 or more)

The Clouds + The Moon + The Coffin

Mental disturbances caused by spirit influences

The Coffin + The Scythe + The Person Card

Violent death

The Coffin + The Star

Psychic abilities are blocked

The Coffin + The Star + The Person Card

Prophetic dreams

The Whip + The Star

Invoking the aid of spirit/prayer

The Fox + The Moon + The Birds + The Whip

Clear-Audible abilities (hearing the voices of spirit)

The Star + The Sun + The Person Card

Clairvoyance (being able to see spirit)

The Star + The Child

Spirit being

The Star + The Mountain

The client's personal Spirit Guide

The Star + The Sun + The Clouds

The world of Spirit

The Star + The Cross

Spiritual evolution

The Person Card + The Sun

Spiritual abilities

The Sun + The Clouds OR The Sun + The Star

Positive spiritual work ('white magic')

The Sun + The Coffin + The Clouds

Negative spiritual influences

The Sun + The Person Card + The Whip

The natural ability to perform spiritual healing

The Moon + The Person Card

Mediumistic abilities

The Scythe + The Coffin + The Cross + The Person Card

Violent death caused by the person's beliefs and ideology in a past life

PART II
SPREADS

The Great Spread

The most famous and also the original spread used by Mlle Lenormand is in this book referred to as The Great Spread (see below). It involved all 36 cards to be laid out in 4 rows of 8 cards each. The remaining 4 cards are laid out below the last row of 8 cards.

As always, shuffle the cards, then let your client shuffle. Take the cards back and see if they 'feel ready', then have the client cut the deck 3 times. Ask which pile to be used first and take this pile back in your hands. Ask the client which pile to be used next and add this pile to the bottom of the cards already in your hand. Then add the last pile again to the bottom of the cards already in your hand. Now flick or tap the middle finger of your other hand 3 times on the back of the pile. The cards are now ready to be laid out face up.

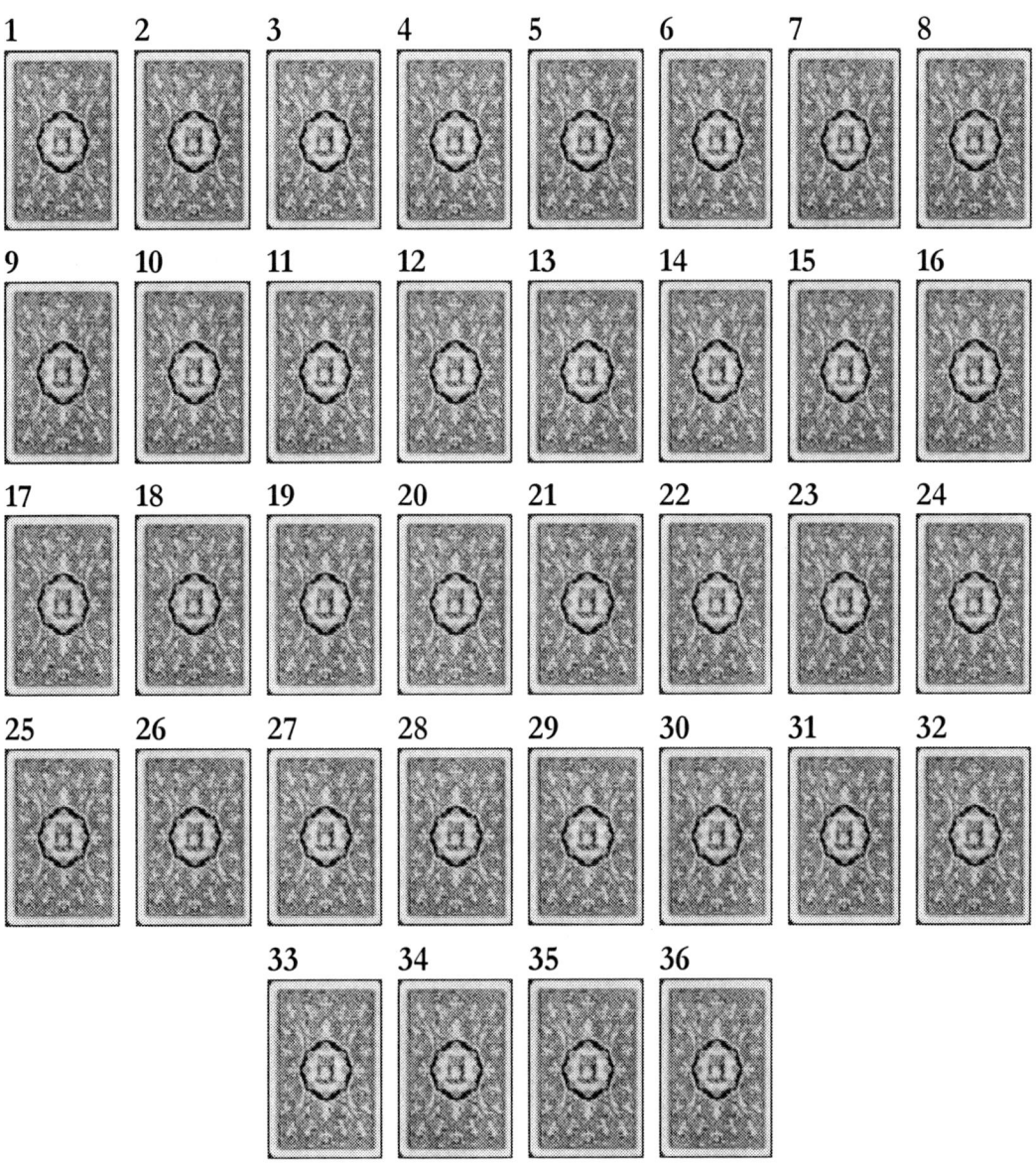

You should begin your reading by finding the Person Card or Indicator Card - see page 125. You would use The Gentleman (card 28) if you read for a male client, The Lady (card 29) if your client is female. Also examine where these two cards are in relation to each other. Some newer Lenormand decks have changed the direction into which either The Gentleman and The Lady 'look', and designed the cards in such as way, that both look in the same direction. This makes professional readings harder and can bring serious confusion. However, according to the old Lenormand cards, the direction into which the cards 'look' indicates what lies ahead of the client. What is shown 'in the back of the Person Card' shows what is in the past of the client. This can be tricky to remember as The Gentleman card looks 'to the right' or in the direction in which the cards are laid out. The Lady looks 'to the left' so to speak!

From my personal experiences and from information obtained from other readers, I can say that 90% of all clients have questions regarding relationships, love and romance. All cards in between The Gentleman and The Lady indicates what 'stands between' the couple. This can be read diagonal as well as vertically. If The Lady and The Gentleman 'look' at each other or 'face' each other, then the couple is very harmonious. If the cards lie 'with their backs to each other' then the couple doesn't have much to say to each other. The card which appears first whilst the cards are laid out is most likely the more dominant partner in the relationship. Don't just look which card comes first to see if the cards face each other or if the cards face away from each other! Draw an imaginary line between the two cards, and see if they face each other or if the look away from each other 'along this line'.

The Moreau Spread

Another interesting and somewhat more challenging spread is the Moreau Spread (see next page), named after Mlle Lenormand's student Adele Moreau. This spread involves only 24 cards, plus either **The Gentleman** if your client is male, or **The Lady**, if your client is female.

Before you start the reading or let the client shuffle, take the Person Card of you client out of the deck - **The Gentleman** if your client is male, or **The Lady**, if your client is female. As always, shuffle all of the remaining 35 cards, then have your client shuffle. Take the cards back to see if the deck 'feels ready', then have the client cut the deck 3 times. Ask which pile to be used first and take this pile back in your hands. Ask the client which pile to be used next and add this pile to the bottom of the cards already in your hand. Then add the last pile again to the bottom of the cards already in your hand. If you are left-handed, you will most likely collect the cards into your right hand. On the contrary, right-handed readers will most likely collect the cards into their left hand. Now flick or tap the middle finger of your other hand 3 times on the back of the pile. The cards are now ready to be laid out in the following way:

Lay out 7 cards, **face down**, and an 8th card at the bottom. Leave enough space to add two more rows. Again, lay out a second row of 7 cards and an 8th card at the bottom, next to the other card you have already laid down at the bottom. Again, add a third row of 7 cards and add the 8th card again to the bottom, next to the other two cards you have already laid out. This gives you 3 rows of 7 cards plus 3 cards at the bottom.

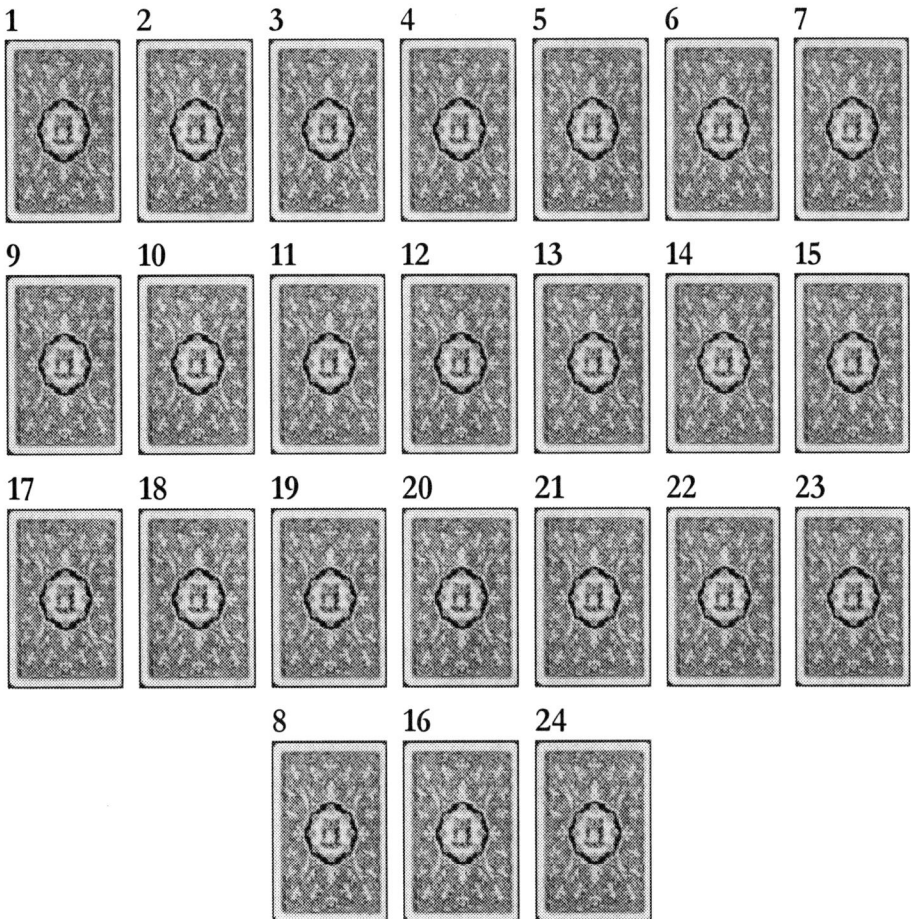

Now add the person card and lay it **face up** on top of the middle card (number '12') - 2nd row, 4th card! The direction into which the cards 'look' indicates what lies ahead of the client. What is shown 'in the back of the Person Card' shows what is in the past of the client.

Three-Dimensional Readings

As mentioned earlier, the most popular and 'traditional' Lenormand spread is The Great Spread, sometimes called The Great Picture. But The Great Spread is more then just a simple way of interpreting card combinations! What follows here is yet another level of interpreting the cards, and moving from two-dimensional left and right interpretations, to interpreting each card for its unique place in the spread – going into a 3rd dimension so to speak! In the Great Spread, all 36 cards are used – 4 rows of 8 cards, plus 4 cards at the bottom. No matter what the first card is you lay out in your reading, it can always be interpreted in combination with **The Cavalier** - card 1 of the deck. In the same aspect, the second card you draw or lay our can be interpreted in combination with **The Clover** - card 2. The third card you lay out or draw can be read in combination with **The Ship** – card number 3, and so on and so forth.

Let me give you an example. In reading for a client and using The Great Spread, the first card laid out is **The Mountain**. You can now interpret **The Mountain** card in combination with

The Cavalier – the first card in the deck! You could tell your client the following: *'Your life is finally improving. After a period of stagnation and slow progress, even after a drought in your life. But your hard work is finally paying off'*.

The next card laid out is **The Dog**. Now interpret this card in combination to **The Mountain**, but also in combination to **The Clover** - card number 2 in the Lenormand deck! You could tell your client the following: *'You have made new friends and acquaintancse a little while ago…'* (**The Dog + The Clover**) *'…who have helped you to overcome these difficulties'* (**The Dog + The Mountain**).

The next card drawn in our example is **The Tree**. By interpreting the combination of **The Tree** and **The Ship** – card number 3 in the deck - but also by incorporating the combination of **The Dog** and **The Tree**, you could tell your client that: *'meeting these new friends and acquaintances was not just simply luck or accident, but predestined!…'* (**The Tree + The Dog**) *'… This friendship will grow and develop and will have a deep impact on your future life'* (**The Tree + The Dog**).

This is a fairly complex way of reading the cards, one I prefer myself. However, it may be advisable to start just on the simple eight card spread then go on to great spread and then delve further into this kind of reading at a later stage.

Simple Eight Cards Spread

Before you start the reading and before you let the client shuffle, take the Person Card of your client out of the deck - **The Gentleman** if your client is male, or **The Lady**, if your client is female. As always, shuffle the remaining 35 cards, then have your client shuffle. Take the cards back to see if the deck 'feels ready', then have the client cut the deck 3 times. Turn each pile over to see the bottom cards. This will already give you some insight into client's situation and the spiritual forces surrounding him or her.

Now put all 3 piles back together into one pile of cards. If you are left-handed, you will most likely collect the cards into your right hand. On the contrary, right-handed readers will most likely collect the cards into their left hand. Now flick or tap the middle finger of your other hand 3 times on the back of the pile. Place the Person Card in front of you. The cards are now ready to be laid out in the following way around the Person Card, face up:

The first card is placed to the left, the second card to the right. The third card above the Person Card, the forth blow and so on following the numbered outline on the next page.

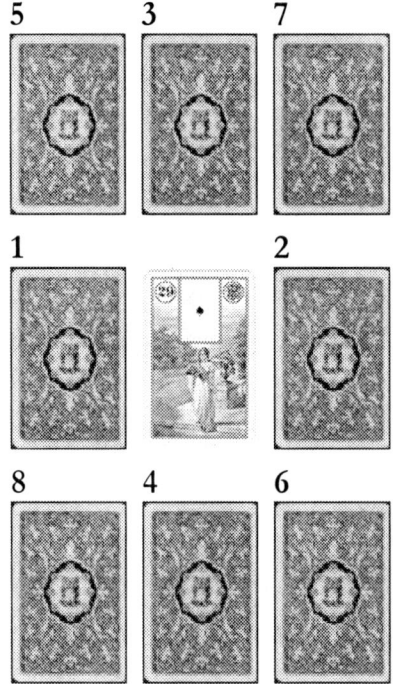

Again the direction into which the cards 'look' indicates what lies ahead of the client. What is shown 'in the back' of the Person Card shows what is in the past of the client.

Hint: Remember that The Gentleman card looks 'to the right'. The client's past would be shown here in cards 1, 5, and 8, the future in cards 7, 2 and 6. Card 3 and 4 show present circumstances and influences.

The Lady looks 'to the left' so to speak! Her past would be shown here in cards 7, 2 and 6. The future is revealed in cards 1, 5, and 8 whilst Card 3 and 4 again show present circumstances and influences

PART III
OTHER ASPECTS OF THE WORK

Divination with the Help of a Gypsy Spirit

The Gypsy people have always been associated with fortune telling and divination - be it as Palm Readers, by the aid of cards, crystal balls, tea leaves or coffee ground. Remembering Mlle Lenormand's affinity with the Gypsy people, it is not surprising to see why her fortune telling cards are often referred to as The Gypsy Cards. In Brazil, among the followers of the Umbanda and Quimbanda traditions*, the Lenormand cards are well known as *O Baraho Cigano* - the Gypsy Deck. Many followers of these traditions believe that it will be beneficial for a person to employ the help of a gypsy spirit in divination also. Umbanda and Quimbanda believe that a person's spirit lives on after death, and that the wisdom and insight of those spirits can open new horizons in working with these cards. Mlle Lenormand after all learned her noble art from the Gypsy people and herself worked with a spirit guide called Ariel.

The work with Gypsy Spirits within Umbanda and Quimbanda is quite old and traditional. It is rare but not uncommon to even see Umbanda Centers across Brazil and other Latin American Countries being dedicated to various Gypsy Spirits. I have also seen references to Gypsy spirits being employed in other African Based traditions outside of Brazil, namely Caribbean Espiritismo and Brujeria/Witchcraft. I even have a Haitian Gypsy Doll among my personal possessions. Called Povo Cigano amongst followers of Umbanda and Quimbanda, the gypsy people are true travelers, free and cheerful, their origin is as we believe in India, but within our tradition we can also see manifestations of these spirits from countries such as Spain, Portugal, Hungary, Morocco,

---

*For more information on Umbanda, see *'Sarava Umbanda – The Inner Workings of Mcumba'* by Mario dos Ventos, Lulu.com, 2007. For further information on Quimbanda, see *'Na Gira do Exu'* by Mario dos Ventos, Lulu.com, 2006.

Algeria, Russia, Romania and Yugoslavia. However most scholars see the origin of the gypsy people in the northwest of India. The reason why these people abandoned their native country is still a mystery though. The general 'feeling' and atmosphere that the Gypsy Spirits bring with them is very exotic, oriental, colorful and musical. Amongst the most common and most well known male Gypsy Spirits in Umbanda are Cigano Pablo, Cigano Wlademir, Cigano Ramirez, Cigano Juan, Cigano Pedrovick, Cigano Artemio, Cigano Hiago, Cigano Igor, Cigano Vitor and many others. Cigana Emerald, Cigana Carmem, Cigana Salomé, Cigana Carmencita, Cigana Rosita, Cigana Madalena, Cigana Yasmin, Cigana Maria Dolores, Cigana Zaira, Cigana Sunakana, Cigana Sulamita, Cigana Wlavira, Cigana Iiarin and Cigana Sarita are some of the most well know manifestations of female Gypsy Spirits. Quimbanda knows Gypsy Spirits such as Pomba Gira Sete Saias, Pomba Gira Menina, Pomba Gira Cigana da Calunga and Pomba Gira Cigana da Praia to only name a few. There is also a clear distinction between the general division of Gypsy Spirits and entities of Quimbanda known as Exu Ciganos (Gypsy Exu) and Pomba Gira Cigana (Pomba Gira Gypsy). Even though there are some Gypsy spirits who manifest within the lines of Exu and Pomba Gira, not all Gypsy spirits are automatically part of the hierarchy of Quimbanda. Exu Ciganos and Pomba Gira Ciganas can be seen as having 'two citizenships'. They are part of the general Division of Gypsy Spirits but are also at home among the Exus and Pomba Giras of Quimbanda. Some followers of Umbanda even teach that those Gypsies who manifest in Quimbanda - a tradition usually seen as much darker and much more earth bound then Umbanda - are 'Guardians of Light within the Darkness'. How true or how overly romantic this idea is should not be discussed here.

The Ceremony

The following ceremony is only a suggestion for anyone interested in tapping into the power of the Gypsy Spirits. It is best performed on a Friday night.

You will need:

- 1 female Gypsy Doll or alternatively a female Flamenco Dancer doll
- 7 red taper candles
- 7 black taper candles
- 1 bottle of Bay Rum
- 1 small bottle of Anisette Liquor
- 1 shot gloss
- 1 square piece of red fabric (preferably silk)
- 1 square piece of black fabric (preferably silk)
- 1 glass ashtray
- 7 fine cigarettes
- 7 One Penny coins
- 7 red roses without thorns
- 1 small glass vase
- Pomba Gira Cigana Oil

Start by laying out the black piece of fabric. Place the red fabric over it to form an 8-pointed star. Next, wash the doll with the Bay Rum. Do this by taking a good amount of the Bay Rum in your hands and 'wash' over the doll. Do the same with the Anisette Liquor.

Now place the doll in the middle of the fabric, on one side of the doll place the vase with 7 roses, on the other side place a glass of Anisette Liquor. Around all this, now place 7 red and 7 black candles alternately until you have formed a circle around the working. These candles as well as the dolls hands, feet and head should beforehand be anointed with Pomba Gira Cigana Oil. Put the ashtray in front of her and light the 7 cigarettes. Don't smoke these cigarettes, but leave them in the ashtray as an offering for the Gypsy spirit you are about to invoke.

Now invoke the Gypsy people. No formal prayers or formulas are needed, simply pray from your heart and ask that one will come to be your guide and to open the mysteries of the cards for you. When the candles have burned down, take the offerings together with 7 pennies to a T-shaped crossroad.

As for the doll, it will represent the Gypsy spirit that you will be working with from now on. Keep her on the fabric you used in the above ceremony, light candles for her and dedicate your divination tools to her. A simple dedication ceremony for the deck is given on page 154. You might want to buy a bottle of perfume for her and spray the statue with it every once in a while. Maybe you find some nice and inexpensive costume jewelry on your next shopping trip, which you might want to dedicate to her and place on her statue. It is also a good idea to keep a glass of fresh water in front of the doll. Change this water every Friday as well as if it gets cloudy and evaporates too quickly.

The next couple of pages will give some more ideas and tips on working with the Gypsy spirits.

'May the Road be gentle to your feet, the wind blow light upon your shoulders,
May the sun shine warm upon your face, the rain fall peaceful unto your encampment!
And may I always rest assured, that the Gods guard you in the palms of their hands'

Gypsy Blessing

Blessing the Deck

Santa Sara Kali
Patroness of the Gypsies

All tools employed for divination and fortune telling are simply just that - tools. What makes cards, shells or any other tool created or found in nature a voice of the divine, is the divine essence bestowed upon it in a consecration ceremony. Simply picking up a deck of cards or some shells or Runes and employing them in divination without proper preparation will not reveal the future. The Lenormand Cards are no exception. In a previous part of this book you have learned how to invoke the help of a Gypsy Spirit in divination. You have been given a ceremony to attract a Spirit Teacher, who will guide you in exploring and understanding these cards. Now is the time to also prepare the deck for its future use. If you have performed the ceremony on page 151, then you already have two pieces of fabric ready - one black and one red. You can use this fabric again for this Blessing Ceremony. Prepare an incense made of one teaspoon of Frankincense and one teaspoon of Myrrh then add 10 drops of Jasmine Essential Oil and 10 drops of Sandalwood Essential Oil. If you like to burn incense in your consultations and work with your Gypsy Teacher, then this mixture can also be used. Additionally to the incense, a herbal infusion should be made. Take 1 tablespoon of each of the following, Rosemary, Cinnamon, Star Anise, Juniper Berries Mandrake Root and Rose petals; boil these ingredients with 2 pints of water in a saucepan for 30 minutes. In addition to the above, you will also need the following materials:

- 1 small red candle
- 1 small black candle
- Pomba Gira Cigana Oil
- 1 Moonstone
- 1 Black Onyx
- 4 Silver Coins

Once the infusion has reached a dark greenish-brown colour, strain the mix. Let it cool, and then wash the Moonstone, the Onyx and the 4 silver coins with it. Now place everything in front of your Gypsy Spirit. Arrange the black piece of fabric on the floor or on the table in front of your Gypsy Shrine. Place the red fabric over it to form an 8-pointed star and light some of the Gypsy Incense you prepared earlier. Light the red candle to the left and the black candle to the right of the fabric. Place the Moonstone with the red candle and the Onyx with the black candle then arrange all 4 coins in a row in front of your Gypsy Doll - two coins facing up, two facing down.

Now would be the best time to call upon your Gypsy Guide, using your own words. Tell her that you are about to prepare your Fortune Telling Cards for the work and ask her to give her blessing and support to what you are about to do.

Fan out the complete deck of cards in front of you and one by one, anoint each card lightly with Pomba Gira Cigana Oil. Only use very little oil as you don't want to damage your cards! It is best to run some oil on your hand first and then to anoint the cards with the residue. Lay the cards again face down in front of your Gypsy Doll. Once you are done and the candles are burnt out, place the 4 silver coins on top of your cards and wrap everything first in your red fabric - as an inner layer - and then additionally in black fabric - as an outer later.

You should always keep the cards, coins and gemstones together and you may also be able to use the 4 coins in divination. They can be used similar to the Chamalongos (rounded coconut shells) of Palo Mayombe*, answering simple yes and no questions presented to your Gypsy Guide with 5 possible combinations. To do this, hold the coins in your hand and address a simple yes or no question to your Gypsy Guide. Now throw the coins in front of shrine – preferably on top of the red and black fabric you keep them in. The answers can be as follows:

> 4 positive sides showing - *yes*
>
> 3 positive sides showing - *rephrase your question as something is missing. You are on the right track but still 'not quite there yet' with your question*
>
> 2 positive sides showing - *definite yes!*
>
> 1 positive side showing – *definite no!*
>
> No positive sides showing - *this is not the time to ask such questions!*

To determine which sides are seen as positive or negative is not as easy to define with the coins as it is with the Chamalongos of Palo Mayombe and not every Gypsy spirit might accept this type of divination. Please don't go out and buy Chamalongos as this has nothing to do with either Umbanda or Quimbanda anymore and would take matters simply too far! If your Gypsy Guide accepts this type of coin divination then ask her to identify which sides she wants to use as 'positive' and which sides she wants to use as 'negative'. If she doesn't want to use Coin divination then simply let the matter rest.

---

*Palo Mayombe is an Afro-Cuban religion based in Bantu/Congo spirituality

Macumba -
Cleaning up the Client's Destiny

Interpreting the Cards the 'Macumba Way'

The first part of the book gave explicit information on the traditional meanings of the Lenormand cards. This section deals with card meanings and interpretations according to Brazilian Umbanda and Quimbanda. Only a small section on this work has been dedicated to these interpretations as an extensive knowledge of these traditions in needed to perform accurate and helpful divination. What is listed here has been listed to give a more complete idea as to how these cards are used in other parts of the world and should serve as an introduction only. The meanings given below as well as the associations with Orixas (spirits of Africa) and other spiritual entities have been passed on to me by a Brazilian Babalorixa friend who is initiated in Umbanda as well as Candomble. It needs to be emphasised that this system of divination as it is presented in this book can not be used to determine a person's Guardian Orixa or personal spirit guide! A great deal of experience as well as proper training and initiation into these traditions is needed to perform such divination!

Serge Bramley in his book *'Macumba' - The Teachings of Marie-José, Mother of the Gods'** gives an excellent introduction to this unique system of Brazilian spirituality. I am also in the process of compiling a thorough manual on Umbanda[2] and two works on the possibilities of working with the sprits of Quimbanda[3]. Macumba is not a valid tradition in itself but a term often used in Brazil to describe African traditions and religions. The term 'Macumba' however is a slang term used as a reference to Congo related magical workings. It is frequently used in Brazil to refer to any ritual or religion of African original though it's generally seen as a derogatory and offensive term. Its modern day meaning is related to negative witchcraft, bindings, curses etc, and the phrase 'doing a

---

* Serge Bramley, *'Macumba - The Teachings of Marie-José, Mother of the Gods'* City Lights, 1994

[2] Mario dos Ventos, *'Sarava Umbanda - The Inner Workings of Macumba'*, Lulu.com 2007

[3] Mario dos Ventos, *'The Black Book of Exu - Tapping into the Power of the Master of Reality'* Lulu.com, 2007 as well as *'The Red Book of Pomba Gira - Tapping into the Power of the Queen of the Night'*, Lulu.com, 2007

Macumba' is generally employed in reference to any kind of witchcraft in Brazil. Macumba -, which interestingly enough derived from the Bantu 'ma-Kiumba' - loosely translates to 'Spirits of the Night'. Reference is here given to the practice of secret, nightly meetings. The word 'Macumba' if used among actual practitioners is not viewed as negative, but its use by non-practitioners remains largely derogatory in intent.

Umbanda and Quimbanda (two of the traditions that are usually referred to as Macumba) are essentially 'spirit religions'. This means that practitioners of these religions seek the aid of these entities in matters of love, health, financial and spiritual success and in all other areas of mundane and spiritual life. The Lenormand cards can give insight as to which entities can be approached for help but also show which spiritual influences should be placated, calmed or even eradicated in a person's life. This form or interpretation is very much linked to a person's destiny of life-path. As mentioned previously in this book, divination should be more then simple 'fortune telling'. It is the art to access divine information related to the client's destiny and life-path. It should help clients to align themselves with their destiny and to achieve a life of health, wealth, happiness and fulfillment. The repertoire of the Macumbeiro, Umbandista or Quimbandeiro not only involved the diagnosis of spiritual problems by the use of divination, but also to provide relief for those same ailments. The following pages contain some recipes for spiritual baths and oils, which can be used and easily amended for a variety of the smaller and greater problems of life. I am well aware that this aspect of the work is not performed by most Western readers and Fortune Tellers. However, this section was added to give those who are looking for 'something more' the opportunity to give extra help to their clients. The information below was not added to increase your income as a Spiritual Worker and Fortune Teller, but simply intended as a help to enrich your work and the lives of your clients.

As mentioned previously in this work, a skilled reader or fortune teller will be able to create a meaningful and clear tapestry, allowing the colors and meanings of individual strands/cards to surface, to be interwoven in a way that can help the client to understand his or her destiny better. Divination after all is more then simple 'fortune telling'. It is the art to access divine information related to the client's destiny and life-path. Every reader or diviner needs to remember, that it is their duty to help their clients to align themselves with their destiny and achieve a life of health, wealth, happiness and fulfillment. If this alignment can not be provided during the ritual of divination, then it is nothing more then a game and useless past time. One form of 're-alignment or re-affirming' a person with his or her destiny is giving them a little push in the right direction using some of the 'Macumbas' (spiritual workings) mentioned below.

Card Meanings

Card 1 – The Cavalier

This card talks about streets and roads, especially in the countryside or generally outside of town or village. It can also be understood as outside our 'natural habitat' or field of action. It is a card of 'open roads' and indicates creativity, new ideas, good luck and the materialization of ideas and projects. It brings with it the capacity to positively change the course of ones life and the course of action in general. The client will achieve his goals and all obstacles will be removed. This card always minimizes the effect of negative cards. Macumba also associates this card with the forces represented by Orixas Oxala and Xangô.

Card 2 – The Clover

Whereas this is usually seen as a symbol of luck and good fortune, the Brazilian meaning is somewhat different. The Clover symbolizes the stumbling blocks, ups and downs, disorientation and worries we encounter in our life. It tells the client that he or she needs some luck to handle the coming obstacles and that he or she should proceed carefully, examine the situation well and only act after thorough consideration of all possibilities. The Clover also tells us that obstacles will not last forever but will pass by. How to determine what is needed for luck to manifest in the client's life and which entities should be approached will be shown on page 166.

Card 3 – The Ship

The raw power of the ocean manifests in this card. Rivers, lakes and the sea show their presence here. Whereas The Cavalier spoke about new possibilities, 'open roads' and the Light at the End of the Tunnel, this card goes a step further. Its message is that it is no longer just possible to improve in life, it is already happening. The client is not there yet, but he or she is very much on the way. Something new has already begun. Being deeply connected with water, this card also tells the client to pay attention to his or her emotions and intuitions. The Ship also brings wealth. Near the Person card it may also indicate a short journey. Macumba also associates this card with the forces of the sea. The Orixa Iemanyá (the queen of the ocean) as well as the Marinheiros (spirits of Sailors and Pirates) influence this card.

Card 4 – The House

The house in relation to the spiritual meaning and interpretation of Macumba, not only indicates the client's own home, but also the company and community of like minded souls. It tells the client that he or she needs to broaden their horizons, go out and seek the company of others instead of isolating themselves. It also challenges the client to take care of his or her spiritual needs better.

Card 5 – The Tree

The Tree is seen as a symbol of progress, fertility, stability and vitality. Near the client, The Tree indicates good luck and progress. It also invites the client to leave his or her fears behind as the fulfillment of his or her happiness and dreams will surely come! Further removed from the Person Card, it speaks of good health. Macumba also associates this card with the forces represented by the Orixa Tempo/Iroko.

Card 6 – The Clouds

Sometimes referred to as 'The Winds', this card speaks of 'cloudiness' in the person's mind and in his or her perception. It warns not to make hasty changes but to tread carefully as the client may easily misunderstand what is said or done. But misunderstandings can also happen the other way round - the client's words and actions might be misunderstood by others. The surrounding cards should be examined closely and clear advice should be given so that the client's life might not 'turn sour'. Macumba also associates this card with the forces which manifest in the air and with quick changes and development.

Card 7 – The Snake

This card usually presents a warning to the client. It tells him or her to carefully examine which people he or she spends time with and advises to stay away from persons of dubious character and from dangerous endeavors. Hypocrisy, lies and falsehood are all around the client if this card appears near him or her. The client is usually advised to look after him or herself better, not to make compromises but to 'clean up' - to create spiritual and physical cleanliness. It is best to avoid dark places, such as night clubs, dark places in bars and restaurants and dark streets. Macumba also associates this card with the forces represented by Orixas Nanã and Oxumare.

Card 8 – The Coffin

Similar to the Death card in the Tarot, The Coffin is a card of initiation, of endings and new beginnings. Also referred to as 'The Candle' by some Brazilian initiates, it speaks also of disturbances caused by spiritual influences - either by the spirits of the dead or by other spiritual entities which ask to be acknowledged and honored. In the cosmology of Brazilian traditions, initiation is seen as one way to overcome these difficulties.

Card 9 – The Flowers

Sometimes referred to as 'The Rain', this card is always a positive omen. It speaks of joy, laughter, generosity and emotional fulfillment. It brings healing to the sick, happiness to lovers and financial profits to merchants. This card also brings the achievement of possibilities and dreams. The other name for this card - The Rain - shows that it indicates spiritual cleansing. Flowers are often used either in spiritual baths or directly on the body to get rid of negative influences and 'spiritual contaminations'. Macumba also associates this card with the forces represented by the Orixa Oxum.

Card 10 – The Scythe

This card speaks of losses and danger. It shows that the client will have to face delicate and difficult situations where he or she will have to accept loss and will have to make compromises to achieve goals. The effects of this card are usually abrupt and unexpected. Just as the scythe of the farmer ends the life-cycle of the corn, so does the corn in turn sustain the life of men by providing food. This speaks of unnecessary attachments and baggage which the client should lose to be able to move forward spiritually. The message that this card brings is that 'now is the time for change'. Macumba also associates this card with the forces represented by the Orixa Omolu and also Iku (death himself).

Card 11 – The Whip

Sometimes referred to as 'The Sword', this card is usually seen as a symbol of difficult situations and oppression. It brings entanglements, discussions and mental tortures as well as strife, discord and disagreements. It asks the client not to use his or her energy for destruction and domination but for his or her spiritual evolution. Some readers also call this card 'The Broom' which shows that it can also initiate a time of spiritual cleansing - a time where the client will be able to see who his or her true friends are! The advice this card brings is to bite one's tongue and to seek the advice of a third party. Macumba also associates this card with the spiritual forces represented by the Orixa Oya/Iansã and by the entity known as Pomba Gira.

Card 12 – The Birds

This is a card of positive developments, of happiness, love, romance and courtship. It brings luck in business and profitable business associations. This card especially neutralizes the influence of The Snake (card 7). Macumba also associates this card with the spiritual forces represented by the Orixa Oxossi and the spirits known as Caboclos (Native American Indians).

Card 13 – The Child

This card represents joy, innocence and spontaneity. It brings originality, kindness and hope. This card points at somewhat unpredictable developments that need close attention. It tells the client to be 'like a child' - to follow his or her course of action without fear or doubt. At the same time it advises not to lose sight of surrounding developments but to be alert, watchful and ready to act. He or she needs to pay close attention to positive opportunities which will present themselves soon. Macumba also associates this card with the spiritual forces represented by the Orixa Ibejis and the entities known as Erês (spirits of children).

Card 14 – The Fox

This card represents disloyalty, traps, falsehoods, lies, envy and cleverness. It warns the client of false proposals and shows that someone might try and involve him or her in a complicated situation - to see the client struggle and fall. The Fox tells the client that salvation will be brought about by being cunning, clever and wise. Macumba also associates this card with the spiritual forces represented by the Orixa Elegbara.

Card 15 – The Bear

The Bear is the card of false joy and false laugher. It does not represent serious danger but simply brings two important messages to the client. Firstly, he or she needs to be alert and on guard. Many people are pleasant and friendly towards the client but their motives are greed and envy. Secondly, the client needs to guard his or her secrets better and not put too much trust and confidence in others. It is best not to share positive or negative events and developments with others but to simply put on a (false) smile and to say that everything is ok, neither good nor bad! This will discourage people's curiosity and many will lose interest in harming the client.

Card 16 – The Star

This card brings luck, success, inspiration and new opportunities. It tells the client that his or her plans and activities are 'under a good star' and that he or she should trust in his or her faith and intuition. Macumba also associates this card with the person's Guardian Angel. Special attention is needed should The Flowers (card 9) appear with The Star. This indicates that the client needs to develop his mediumistic abilities and involve him or herself more deeply with spiritual matters.

Card 17 – The Stork

This is the card of the un-expected - be it unexpected new or surprising developments. It represents the need and the desire for change. It symbolizes our need not to fall into routines but to 'keep moving'. The Stork always tells us that the 'roads are open' and that we should not allow our own fear to hinder us from moving forward.

Card 18 – The Dog

Fidelity, friendship, companionship and trust manifest in this card. It reminds us that we are surrounded by real and loyal friends and that we can trust them. The Dog also tells us that we are safe and protected. However, should The Clouds (card 6) appear nearby, then this speaks about imbalances in the matters of love and relationships. Macumba also associates this card with the spiritual forces represented by the Orixa Ogum

Card 19 – The Tower

The Tower makes a connection to our interior world and speaks about our spiritual elevation. It indicates that we should give more attention to the world of Spirit, that we should retreat, meditate and develop a close connection to our Higher Self. It shows us that the answers we seek can be found within, by listening to the voice of spirit and by silencing the many voices of the outside world.

Card 20 – The Garden

This card speaks about community and family - our birth family as well as religious family. All Afro-Brazilian traditions are in essence family traditions. There are no solitary practitioners and no self-initiation or self-dedication. The message of this card is to share our sorrows and our joy with others as we are not able to carry our burdens alone. Sorrows shared with others will make them smaller, but joy and happiness shared will multiply. Macumba also associates this card with the spiritual forces represented by the Gypsy spirits.

Card 21 – The Mountain

The Mountain indicates blockages, challenges and difficulties that need to be overcome. But it also stands for stability, firmness and perseverance. This card challenges us to be conscious of our own limits but also of our abilities! It tells us to be resourceful and humble. It can also warn us that unpleasant confrontations might be on their way and advises us to avoid strife and stubbornness. The Mountain helps us to understand when to fight and when to live in peace, when to attack and when to defend ourselves. Macumba also associates this card with the spiritual forces represented by the Orixa Oxalá.

Card 22 – The Ways

This card speaks about choices and determination – 'where there is a will there is a way!' It shows us that there are different possibilities to reach our goal and asks us to search for alternative roads. It is always our choice to either stand-still and stagnate, or to move forward in life - or even to go backwards. This card tells us 'look how far you have come!' and opens the possibility for new endeavors and adventures. Macumba also associates this card with the spiritual forces represented by the entities Exu and Pomba Gira and the forces of Quimbanda

Card 23 – The Mouse

This card warns of loss, sickness and disease. It also shows that something or someone is draining our energy and is 'eating us up on the inside'. The Mouse tells us to take good care of our health and to protect our properties and belongings - material as well as spiritual! We should not allow people to depend on us too much and to drain our physical and spiritual/emotional resources but to show appreciation for what we have. The message of this card is 'You don't know what you have 'till it's gone'. Macumba also associates this card with the spiritual forces represented by the Orixa Elegbara but also with Pomba Gira Maria Mulambo.

Card 24 – The Heart

The Heart speaks about emotions, joy, happiness and harmony. Happy endings, unexpected help and exceptionally lucky circumstances manifest in this card. It also tells us that the 'Matters of the Heart' are not limited to romantic endeavors but also incorporate brotherly love. This card advises us always to lend a helping hand to others and to share our love and joy with the world around us. In return it promises that we will receive help and support when ever we need it.

Card 25 – The Ring

The Ring is always a positive card and brings unity, relationships, marriages as well as all kinds of positive associations. It tells us that relationships will grow stronger and also brings rewarding alliance in matters of business and money. It is very important to also examine the surrounding cards to see exactly what type of connections and relations this card indicates. Macumba also associates this card with the spiritual forces represented by all female Orixas and in particular the Orixa Obbá.

Card 26 – The Book

This is the card of secrets and of knowledge. Unused and unexplored possibilities also manifest here. This card tells us that we need to learn and study to be able to fulfill out destiny. This can either indicate further education at the university or community college or spiritual apprenticeship with a teacher. It shows us that knowledge alone is useless. Insight and wisdom as to how to practically apply this knowledge is also needed. Macumba also associates this card with the spiritual forces represented by spirits such as the Orixa Omulo and especially entities such as the Preto Velhos (spirits of Old Black Slaves) as well as Exu Caveira and the family of 'Cemetery Spirits'.

Card 27 – The Letter

News from distant lands, important papers, documents and invitations to parties manifest in this card. But The Letter not only symbolizes the written word. It can also indicate messages and information that are passed on by word of mouth. It tells us to pay close attention to words and advises to check paperwork carefully before we sign. The nature of the news or message will be determined by the surrounding cards.

Card 28 – The Gentleman

No matter if we are reading the cards 'the Macumba way' or traditional, this card will always be the Person Card if we are reading for a male client. It is also used to indicate the client's partner/spouse if we are reading for a woman.

Card 29 – The Lady

No matter if we are reading the cards 'the Macumba way' or traditional, this card will always be the Person Card if we are reading for a female client. It is also used to indicate the client's partner/spouse if we are reading for a man.

Card 30 – The Lily

Also known as 'The River', this card brings with it peace and tranquility, purity and virtue. It indicates a positive and constructive phase and promises financial and emotional stability and positively influences all other cards in the game. Macumba also associates this card with the spiritual forces represented by the Orixas Oxum and Logum Edé

Card 31 – The Sun

Energy, strength, creativity, prosperity as well as spiritual growth and even pregnancy manifest in this card. The Sun tells us that we can now enjoy 'the sunny side of life'. Smooth developments and a clear and sturdy path are ahead of us. Macumba also associates this card with the divine and the presence and blessings of god.

Card 32 – The Moon

Known as the Card of Honor, The Moon is closely associated with mysticism and hidden, esoteric knowledge. It brings with itself supernatural gifts and intuition and encourages us to follow our spiritual calling. It tells us to pay close attention to our dreams and to follow our sixth sense. The manifestation of this card is two-fold. It incorporates the desire to express ourselves, to enjoy life to the fullest and to experience adventures and ecstasy. But it also draws us into meditation and arouses our desire to dream, to rest and to find comfort. Macumba also associates this card with the forces of the night and with Quimbanda - which is generally seen as raw and aggressive magic.

Card 33 – The Key

This card literally presents us with the key to unlock out hidden resources of strength, courage and knowledge. It tells us move forward without fear or doubt as success is in our reach and difficulties will soon be overcome and forgotten. The Key also asks us not to compromise ourselves or our highest ideals. It tells us that the tests ahead of us can only be mastered with honesty and integrity. To abide by our standards and principles will bring us lasting success and recognition!

Card 34 – The Fishes

Prosperity and abundance - spiritually as well as materialistically - manifest in this card. New ideas and a wealth of energy can bring great success. This card promises general well-being, happiness and contentment. Macumba also associates this card with the forces of water. The Orixas Iemanyá (the queen of the ocean) and Oxum (the Orixa of fresh water) manifest their presence in this card.

Card 35 – The Anchor

This card brings stability and security in all areas of life. It promises health, wealth, happiness and fulfillment. The Anchor tells us that we will soon find a safe haven where we can enjoy a good life on dry land - without storms, trials and tribulations. Macumba also associates this card with the forces of the deep sea, the Orixa Olókum (the Orixa at the bottom of the ocean) as well as the entities known as Marinheiros (spirits of Sailors and Pirates)

Card 36 – The Cross

This card indicates the sufferings, trials and tribulations of life and speaks of suffering, pain and personal failure. It tells us that we are not following our destiny as closely as we should and encourages us to examine our life and priorities very closely. The Cross also indicates an important test and life-lesson. Our actions and reactions determine our future and will shape our happiness and contentment. Macumba also associates this card with the spiritual forces represented by the Preto Velhos (spirits of Old Black Slaves) and by the division of Exus and Pomba Giras known as the 'Cemetery People'.

Going into more detail

The Great Spread as shown on page 145 is by far the most common way of laying out the Lenormand Cards. But employing card divination in 'the Macumba way', we can go one step further. As previously mentioned, Umbanda and Quimbanda are 'spirit religions'. This means that the influence and intervention of certain spiritual entities is sought in matters of love, health, financial and spiritual success and in all other areas of mundane and spiritual life. The Lenormand cards can give insight as to which entities can be approached for help, but also show which spiritual influences should be avoided, calmed or even eradicated in a person's life.

Every problem in life can be seen as involving spiritual influences. *"Hold on here!"* some readers might say..."*What about problems caused by negligence, laziness or simple ignorance?*" Of course this is possible and the statement that all problems and troubles in a person's life involve spiritual influences should not be misunderstood! Even though people can be the root of their own problems, their own negligence, laziness and ignorance can then attract spiritual influences which might hinder them from breaking these negative influences and from moving forward in life. This concept and cosmology ties in with the belief that divination is first and foremost used to help people align themselves with their destiny and to achieve a life of health, wealth, happiness and fulfillment. The skilled reader, be it a Western Fortune Teller or a Macumbeiro, Umbandista or Quimbandeiro trained in the Afro-Brazilian traditions, not only uses these cards to diagnose spiritual imbalances, but is also able to provide relief and to bring a person 'back on track' with their destiny. This fact can not be stressed enough!

The following method of detecting which influences and spirits are at work should only be applied after you have begun working with your Gypsy Guide as outlined from pages 149 onwards. Even though it is the physical cards who allow us to see these influences, it is only by the aid of spirit guides from the above mentioned traditions that the forces at work can be truly detected. It would be quite useless to employ divination and to try and detect these influences without such guides. Logically speaking, someone who does not understand Chinese medicine will also not be able to effectively diagnose any imbalance of Yin and Yang in a person's body and soul and will therefore not be able to make any treatments according to this particular medical system. Following this line of thought, a spirit guide from the Macumba traditions will be the only reliable source to point out which Macumba-related forces are at play in the person's life.

A good mediumistic connection to your Gypsy Guide as well as well developed spiritual intuition is essential to perform this type of 'spiritual diagnosis' effectively. Once imbalances have been detected using The Great Spread plus the meanings and interpretations given above, you would then use your intuition to select an appropriate number of cards from the already laid-out game. These cards will then be given to the client who is advised to shuffle and to place the cards face down on top of the 'detected imbalances'.

The same method can also be applied for the Eight Card Reading mentioned on page 146. Here's an example:

The above spread shows that our female client is about to encounter problems at the workplace. This is indicated by **The Mountain** (card 21) and **The Anchor** (card 35). It is even possible for the client to lose her job – **The Mouse** (card 23) showing losses. All three cards 'in the back' of the client, meaning **The Scythe** (card 10), **The Moon** (card 32) and **The Coffin** (card 8) speak about spiritual attacks and black magic - for lack of a better term. **The Star** (card 16) and **The Coffin** (card 8) in relation to each other also show that the client is feeling dizzy and that she is not able to think clearly at the moment. Her perception of the world around her are very much clouded and she feels as if she is constantly 'living in a fog'.

Working with this particular spread, the reader would then fan out all remaining cards in front of him or herself - the cards still facing down - and would then begin placing additional cards on top of the already existing picture.

Using intuition as well as the information obtained from this book, the reader can then see the following: **The Clover** (card 2) showing that the Client's luck can be restored. **The Flowers** (card 9) and **The Ways** (card 22) showing what is needed for the client to improve her luck and to prevent further harm. These two cards show that the client should go and approach an entity which lives at the Crossroads. This would in most Afro-Brazilian cases be Exu and Pomba Gira. Here is where the reader will have to use his or her intuition! The client could either present a gift of flowers whilst asking the spirits of the crossroads for help and support or she could cleanse herself with these flowers asking that all negative influences will be removed from her.

Much more information about this deep and complex way of working can be found in *'The Red Book of Pomba Gira - Tapping into the Power of the Queen of the Night'* and in *'The Black Book of Exu - Tapping into the Power of the Master of Reality'* as this present volume is intended to deal firstly with divination and fortune telling using the Lenormand Cards and not so much with the workings of Quimbanda.

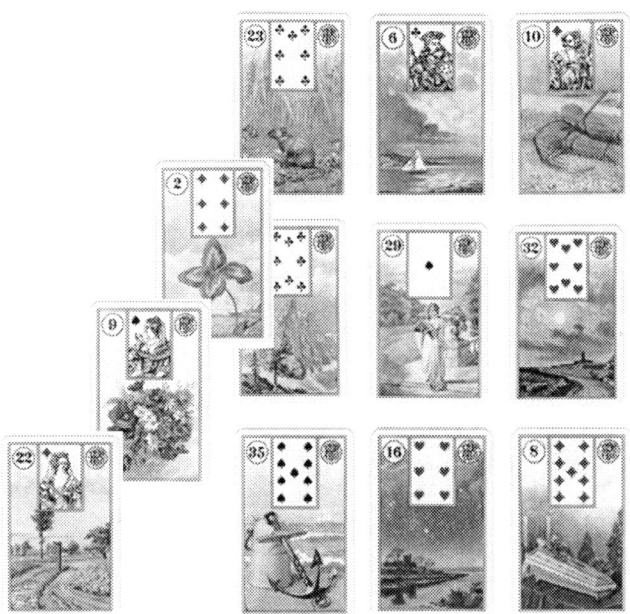

What needs to be remembered when dealing with card interpretations and card divination within the context of Quimbanda and Umbanda is that these religions are not static. Neither are they completely set in stone. The personal experiences and spiritual attunement of the initiate will always influence the quality of the reading. Mediumship development - for lack of a better term - is of utmost importance in this type of divination. The reader will not only have to remember the meaning of the cards but also needs to have a close connection to the spirit world to clearly examine the client's situation. A deep knowledge and understanding of the spirit world is needed to not only identify the forces at play but also to determine appropriate ways to bring about needed changes and developments.

Help Yourself

Many spiritual workers, mediums and fortune tellers, as well as spiritual healers I have encountered over the last couple of years suffer not only from burn-out, but also complain about serious physical and emotional problems. This can extend from actual illnesses - the most common being headaches, back and joint problems as well as insomnia - to difficulties in their marriage and relationships. Not being able to shut out unwanted influences brought into our lives by clients can be the cause of many such problems. No matter if you receive clients at home, in a shop or market stall, it is always recommended to protect the environment, in which you work and live. It is always a good idea to keep a glass of fresh, cool water in the table when doing readings. This serves as refreshment for the spirits that aid us in divination and will also absorb some of the 'negative vibes' some clients might bring with them. To keep a glass of water by the front door will serve the same effect. Some readers will change the water on the table for each new clients and the water by the front door at the end of the day. Another 'trick' is to keep a green coconut by your front door. This will serve the same effect as the glass of water and should be changed monthly. Some clients react negative and even allergic to incense, but a glass of water and a coconut should not provoke such reactions.

Attracting Clients

Advertisements in Local Newspapers and on the Internet can attract clients, however the most powerful tool for attracting clients is, of course, word of mouth, as you then know people respect and trust your readings, also proving to yourself you have the gift of 'reading the cards'. However, should you be working with a Gypsy Spirit then here are two little 'tricks' you can use to attract more clients.

1.) Floor Washes

Prepare a herbal infusion made of Cinnamon stick, Star Anise, red Rose Petals and Roiboos tea. Strain the mixture into a bowl, let it cool down - either cover the bowel or add a wooden spoon to it - and add some Sandalwood Water. Now cover the bowl with a plate and place it in front of your Gypsy doll. Light a candle on top of the plate and ask your Gypsy Spirit to bring more clients to you. Wash your doorstep with the mixture once the candle has burned down.

2.) Small Offerings

Another way of attracting clients with the help of your Gypsy Spirit is to offer her small gifts when ever a new client comes for a reading. Light a candle to your Gypsy on a Friday night, sit in front of the doll for a while and then ask her to increase your clientele over the next weeks and months. Simply promise her a nice piece of costume jewelry, a nice red lipstick or some perfume - Gypsy Spirits are usually quite fond of 'Anise-Anise' Perfume - as soon as you can see an increase of clients. Make sure to keep your end of the bargain.

Below are two 'simple tricks' that can be used to 'recharge' and to get rid of unwanted influences.

1.) Cleansing Bath

Spiritual baths are of utmost importance in Afro-Brazilian traditions. Normally taken cold and poured over the body from the shoulders down, this bath can also be taken hand-warm in the bathtub. All you need is 3 cups of Goats Milk, ¼ cup of Florida Water and a good amount of Lavender Bath Salt. Alternatively to the Lavender salt, you can also use Epsom Salt and Lavender essence.

It is not recommended to dry yourself off after spiritual baths. However, to rid yourself of all negativity, I would recommend using a fresh towel after the bath to 'rub off' all unwanted influences of the day.

2.) Florida Water

This cologne can easily be found in Hispanic or Caribbean beauty shops - no need to run to expensive New Age or Spiritual Supply stores! The scent reminds of Bergamot Oil and of one of the oldest colognes ever to be made - Germany's *4711 Echt Koelnisch Wasser*. Florida Water is used a lot in Caribbean and Afro-American spiritual practices but less common in Brazilian Umbanda and Quimbanda. However, its cleansing effects are truly remarkable and should not be overlooked by any spiritual worker or reader.

It is always good to keep some Florida Water handy and to refresh your forehead and the back of your neck if you 'get stuck' in a reading or feel that the client's questions - or its trying characteristics - 'block' your ability to read. You can also use some of it to cleanse yourself if you cannot afford to take a spiritual bath every day. Either use a couple of splashes on your hands and rub the essence over your head, shoulders, the back of your neck and the front of your body, or mix some of it with fresh water and cleanse yourself and your work area with a damp cloth.

Taking care of your Clients

The cosmology of most African based religions and traditions is based on the concept that a blessing as well as a warning can be foretold by divination. It is then up to the reader or diviner to recommend remedies to either 'secure' the blessing or 'soften' the warning. The following recipes can be used as 'Spiritual First Aid' if it is not possible to help the client by sending him or her to a more experienced spiritual worker.

Spiritual Baths

Spiritual baths are an important part of many spiritual practices, be it Brazilian Umbanda or Quimbanda, Cuban Santeria, Haitian Vodou or Hoodoo and Rootwork of the southern states of the US and the Caribbean. The tradition of baths can also be seen in Medieval European Witchcraft and old European Pagan Traditions. The saying *"cleanliness is goodliness"* surely applies to a person's physical as well as spiritual body alike. Many spiritually minded people as well as many practitioners of various western spiritual traditions easily overlook the beneficial effects of spiritual baths and sometimes seem to care little about spiritual cleanliness in general. The energies we carry around send out signals as to what we wish to attract. People who carry negativity with them will certainly have a hard time attracting good luck and positive changes into their lives. On the contrary, people who carry positive energies with them and send out positive messages to the world around them will definitely find that luck and chance are on their side. Spiritual baths can imprint the person's spiritual body - or Aura for lack of a better term - with certain information. To prepare a spiritual 'Love-Drawing Bath' for example will send the message to the world that the person who applied the bath to his or her body is looking for romantic engagements. A spiritual bath for Protection on the other hand will reinforce the person's spiritual body or Aura which will send out signals of protection and spiritual defense.

Spiritual baths can be applied in two different ways. The traditional way of taking a spiritual bath is to prepare everything in a bowl or bucket and to simply poor the bath over the body once it is ready. Such baths should always be taken cold and the person should always air-dry afterwards. These baths are usually made of fresh herbs and flowers. The second type of bath - and not always the more favorable - is to prepare the actual spiritual bath by boiling the herbs and materials and to immerse oneself and soak in the bath tub. The person should always air-dry afterwards.

Cleansing Bath

Most spiritual problems and blockages in the client's live can easily be cleared by using a spiritual Cleansing Bath. The most basic of these baths can be made in the following fashion:

You will need:

- 6 pints of Water
- 1 pint of Goats Milk
- White Carnations
- A handful of fresh Basil
- Florida Water
- 1 tablespoon of Sea Salt (approx)

Prepare the bath by filling a bowl or bucket with water. Add the Goats milk, then the petals of several carnations. Now mix everything very well together. Some people compare preparing spiritual baths with washing laundry. The flower petals need to be squeezed, torn and mashed together very well. Florida Water and the Sea Salt are added last. The mixture should then be covered with a white towel and a white candle should be lit next to the container. Once the candle has burned out, the client should then pour the bath over their body and air-dry. It is of course not necessary for the client to take any type of spiritual bath at the diviner or fortune teller's home or consultation office. Any bath can, once it is prepared, ready and bottled be given to the client to apply at their own home.

Protection Baths

Are slightly more difficult to prepare but can prove to be very useful should the divination session show any type of concerning or worrying situations in the client's future. The following bath is under the patronage of St Michael the Archangel and can either be taken cold, poured over the body or as a sitting-bath in the bathtub. You will need:

- 10 pints of Water
- 1 red Bell Pepper
- 7 whole Star Anise

- 3 Cinnamon Sticks

- 7 Cloves

- Patchouli Root

- 1 glass of sweet red wine

All ingredients are boiled in a large pot for 45 minutes and then strained.

Love Drawing Baths

These baths are among the most prominent and most often asked-for spiritual baths. The Love Drawing Bath listed here should again be taken cold. This bath can also be put under the patronage of your Gypsy Guide should you be working with one. You will need:

- 6 pints of water

- 1 shot glass of Orange Blossom water

- 1 shot glass of Rose Water

- 5 table spoons of honey

- Yarrow Leaves

- The yellow petals of 2 large sun flowers

(- the petals of 1 red rose, should you be working with a Gypsy Spirit)

This bath is prepared and applied in the same way as the cleansing bath, remembering to squeeze and mash the flower petals.

Luck & Road Opening Bath

African traditions know many different recipes for luck and road opening baths. The simple Luck Bath given here should be prepared with fresh herbs and taken cold, poured over the body. You will need:

- Fresh Rosemary

- Fresh Basil

- Fresh Mint

- ¼ cup of beer or lager

- 2 teaspoons of honey

- Sandalwood Water

- Rose of Jericho Water

After preparation, similar to the cleansing bath listed above, this bath should also be covered with a white towel and a white candle should be lit next to the container and as mentioned before the client then pours the bath over their body and air-dries.

Oils

Sometimes it might be too inconvenient for client's to take spiritual baths - be it related to the person's domestic circumstances or to his or her hectic lifestyle. If the client is for any reason not able to set some time of their day apart for spiritual baths, then Oils and Perfumes can also be used. These can either be worn on the body or applied to amulets and talismans or on the doors and windows in the person's home. I am personally however not aware of any Cleansing Oils and would always advise my own client to do their utmost to at least make time to take a cleansing bath in the evening before bed.

The simple Oil recipes below are designed for Master Bottles which the practitioner should keep in his or her own possession. Portions of these oils can always be given to clients in small Bottles. Should you work with a Gypsy Spirit, then you can also keep these oils on your Gypsy Shrine.

Love Drawing Oil

This oil should be prepared in a red, pink or yellow glass bottle. It is best to either use Sunflower or Sweet Almond Oil as a base. To 100ml of base oil is added Patchouli Essential Oil, Rose Essential Oil, Violet Essential Oil, Orange Blossom Oil and some drops of Molasses. The amount of the other Oils depends on the strength of the individual essential oils. It is also advisable to add 1 small piece each of Liquorice Root, Palo Abre Camino and Palo Amanza Guapo. This oil should rest for 21 days before it can be used.

Love Perfume

A more personalized version of the above Love Drawing Oil is to use the client's favourite perfume and to infuse it with 1 small piece each of Liquorice Root, Palo Abre Camino and Palo Amanza Guapo. The perfume should be allowed to rest for 21 days before it can be used. All 3 ingredients can be left in the bottle until it runs out. More perfume can be added if need be.

Money Drawing Oil

This Oil should be prepared in either a green or brown glass bottle. Jojoba Oil or a mix of ¾ Sweet Almond Oil and ¼ Saffron Oil would be best to use as the base oil. To 100ml of base oil add Cinnamon Essential Oil, Cedar Oil and Sandalwood Essential Oil. The amount of the essential oils depends on the strength of the individual essential oils. The Master Bottle should also contain Palo Abre Camino, Palo Para Mi and 7 grains of Frankincense and 7 Mustard Seeds, again this oil should rest for 21 days before it can be used.

Success Oil

Sometimes called Crown of Success, it is best to use simple Sweet Almond Oil for this mixture. Also add Frankincense Essential Oil, Sandalwood Essential Oil and Vetivert Essential Oil. The amount of these essential oils depends on the strength of the individual essential oils. To the Master Bottle is also added 3 Bay Leaves and 1 whole High John the Conqueror Root. This oil should rest for 28 days before it can be used.

Protection Oil

The Master Bottle of this Oil should be either red or brown and it is best to use Jojoba Oil as a base. Blend Dragon's Blood Essential Oil, Frankincense Essential Oil, Myrrh Essential Oil and add Palo Vence Batalla as well as one branch of dried Rosemary without leaves. The amount of the essential oils depends on the strength of the individual essential oils. This oil should rest for 28 days before it can be used.

Ready Made Formulas

Many spiritual supply stores and Caribbean Botanicas carry a wide range of ready-made oil, powders, baths and even aerosol sprays for all kinds of spiritual ailments and purposes. Most of these formulas used to be very useful and of good quality, but their quality over the last decade or so has unfortunately very much decreased. Most large manufacturers have started to use saw dust and cheap synthetically made oils instead of quality ingredients. What used to be quality-labeled products are now unfortunately only mass-produced curiosities to fool the untrained and naïve community! Some small, independent manufacturers however still produce effective ready-made formulas. What follows is only a hand full of good manufacturers who's products have proved to be good quality and spiritually useful. This list is in no way conclusive!

> Erzulie's Botanica,
>
> *www.erzulies.com*

This online store carries a variety of spiritual soaps which my own guides have advised clients to use.

> The Lucky Mojo Curio Company,
>
> *www.luckymojo.com*

I have personally never purchased any products from this manufacturer but have spoken to other spiritual workers who would recommend some of the materials sold by Lucky Mojo. Of special interest is the owner's book *'Hoodoo Herb and Root Magic'* which gives useful information on the spiritual use of herbs.

> Botanica Maria Padilha,
>
> *www.botanica.moonfruit.com*

This is my own online Botanica. All available formulas are hand made and of good quality ingredients.

There are certainly other small manufacturers who also produce good quality 'spiritual aids'. If you are working with a Gypsy Spirit or other spirit guides in your readings and other spiritual work, then best to check and see if your guides will accept these ready made formulas or if they prefer for you to get your hands dirty, preparing your own oils, powders and baths! Again, it is best to check with your own guides to see of they will recommend the use of any ready-made product.

PERSONAL NOTES

PERSONAL NOTES

PERSONAL NOTES

The Great Spread

Name:...................... Date:..................

Basic Interpretation:
....
....
....
....
....
....
....
....

The Great Spread

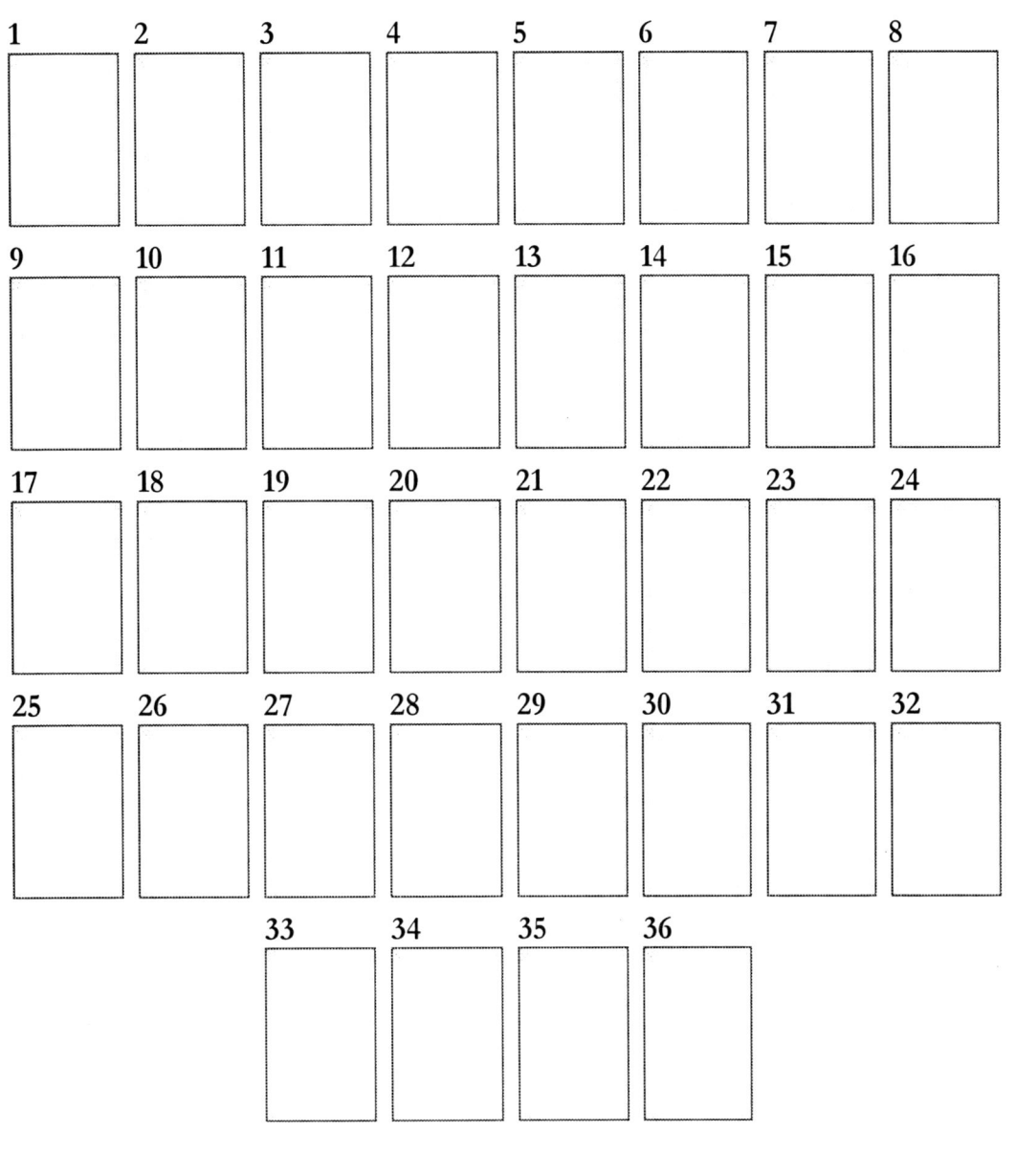

Name:....................   Date:..................

Basic Interpretation:
....
....
....
....
....
....
....
....

The Great Spread

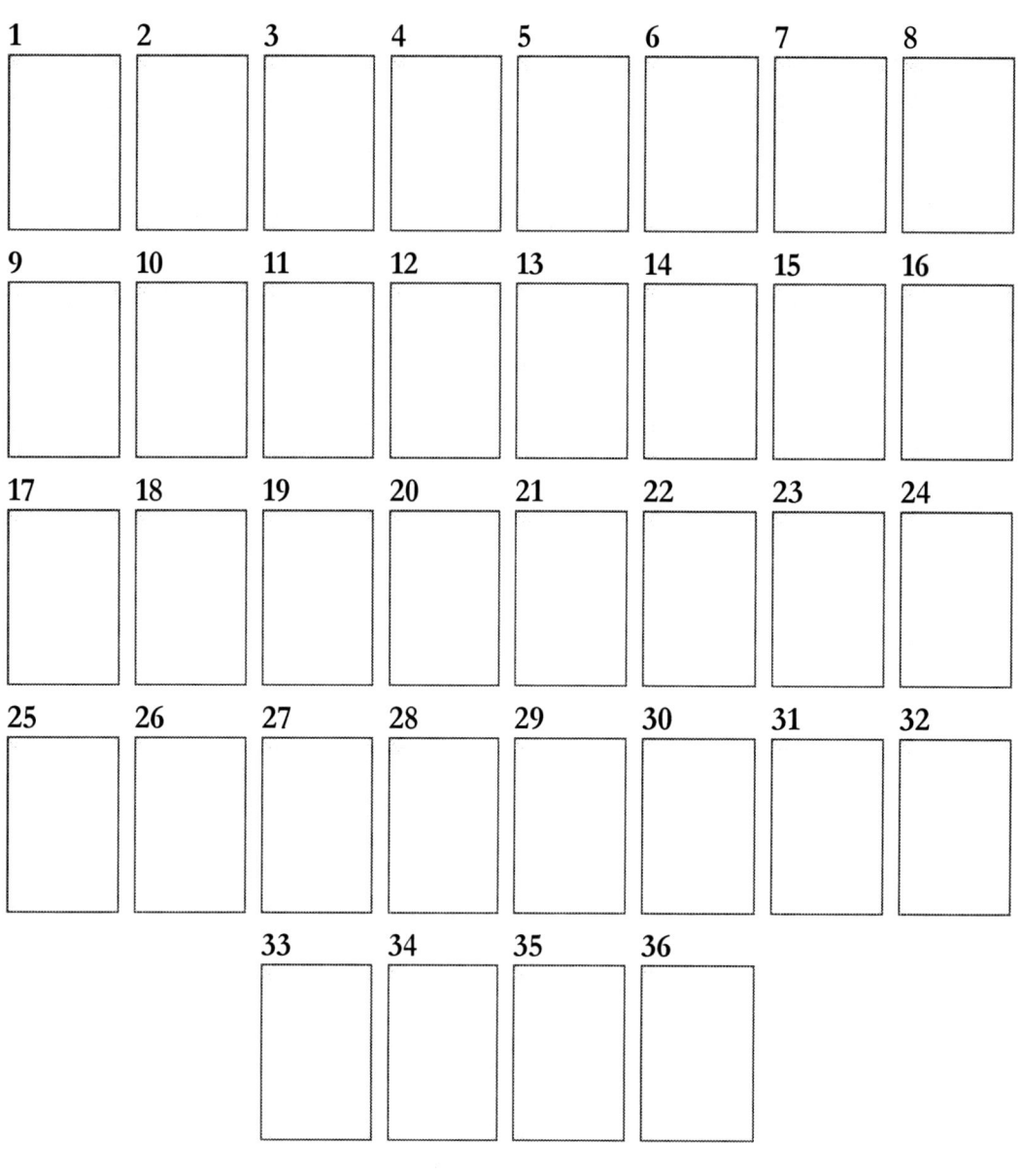

Name:................ Date:................

Basic Interpretation:
....
....
....
....
....
....
....
....

The Great Spread

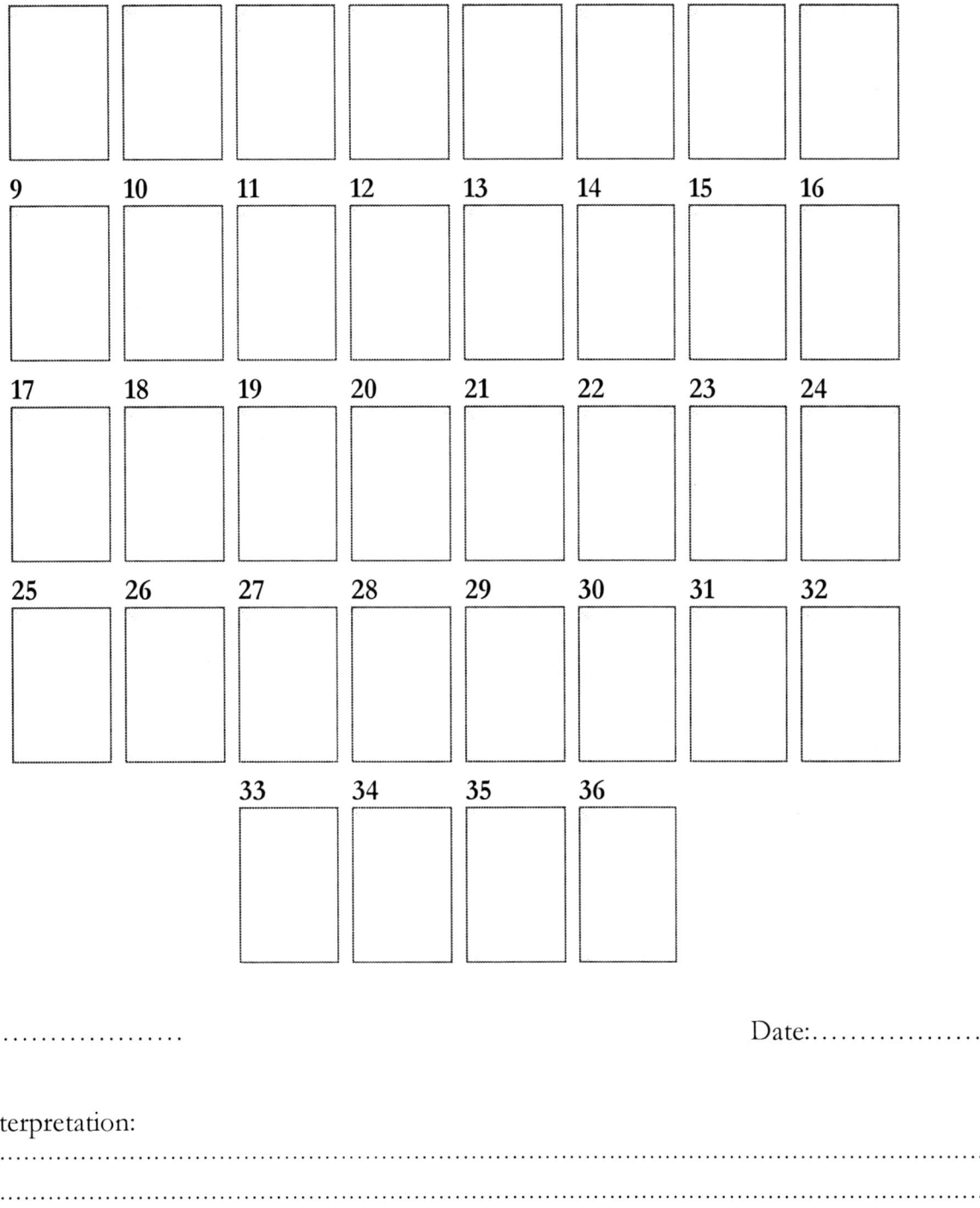

Name:................... Date:..................

Basic Interpretation:
....
....
....
....
....
....
....
....
....

The Moreau Spread

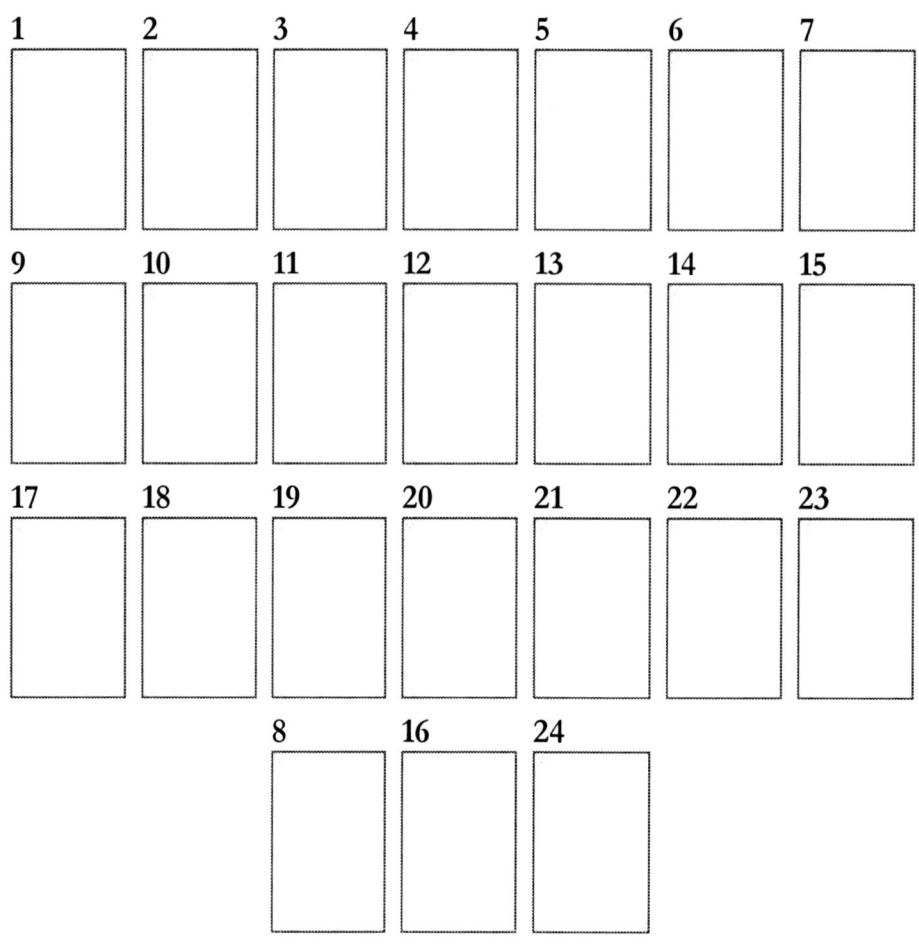

Name:...................   Date:..................

Basic Interpretation:
....
....
....
....
....
....
....
....
....
....

The Moreau Spread

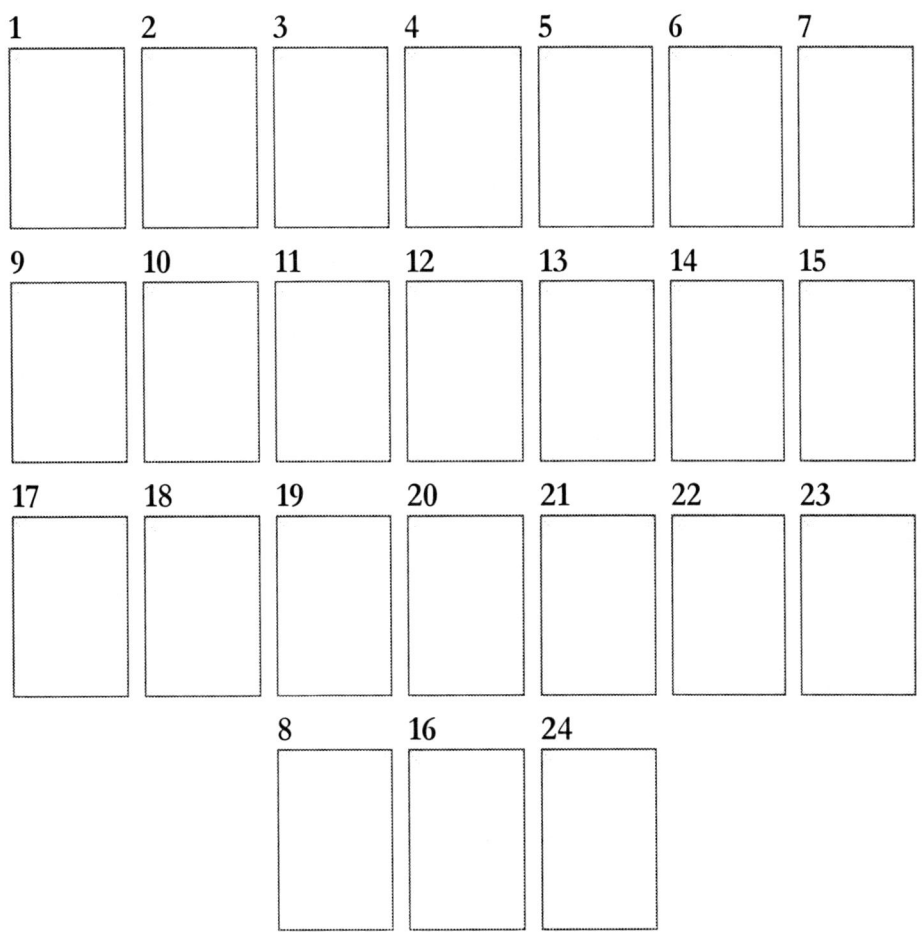

Name:.................... Date:..................

Basic Interpretation:
....
....
....
....
....
....
....
....
....
....

The Moreau Spread

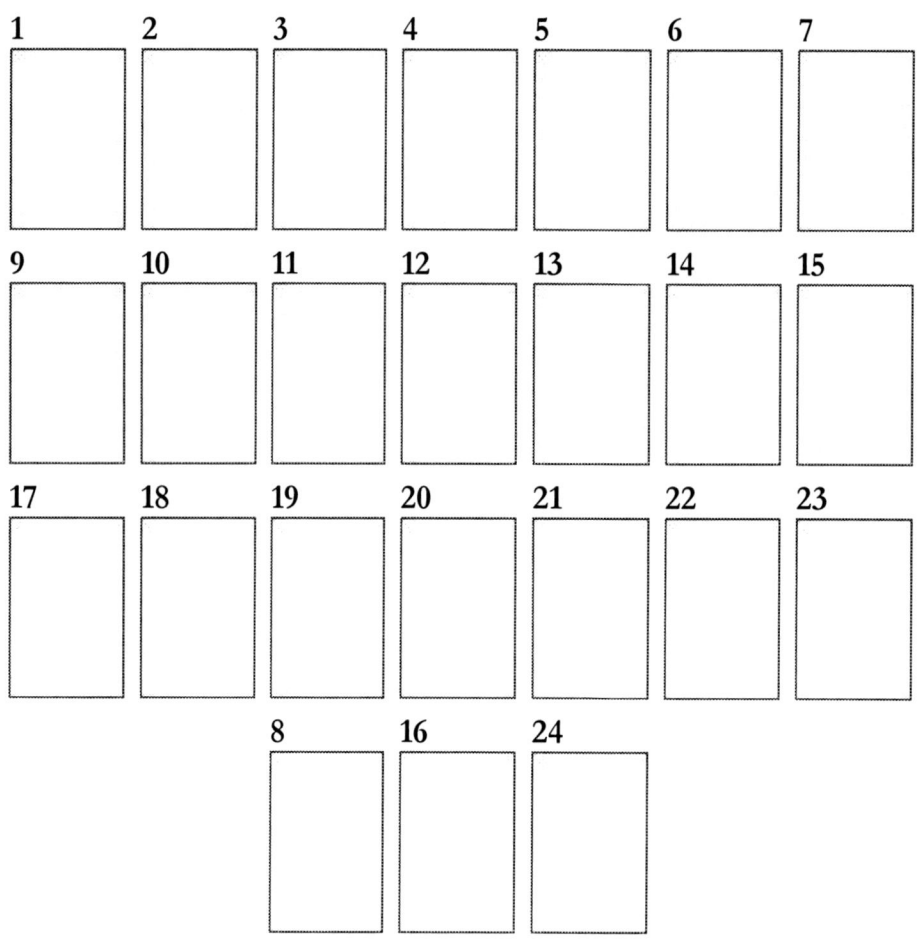

Name:................ Date:..................

Basic Interpretation:
....
....
....
....
....
....
....
....
....
....

The Moreau Spread

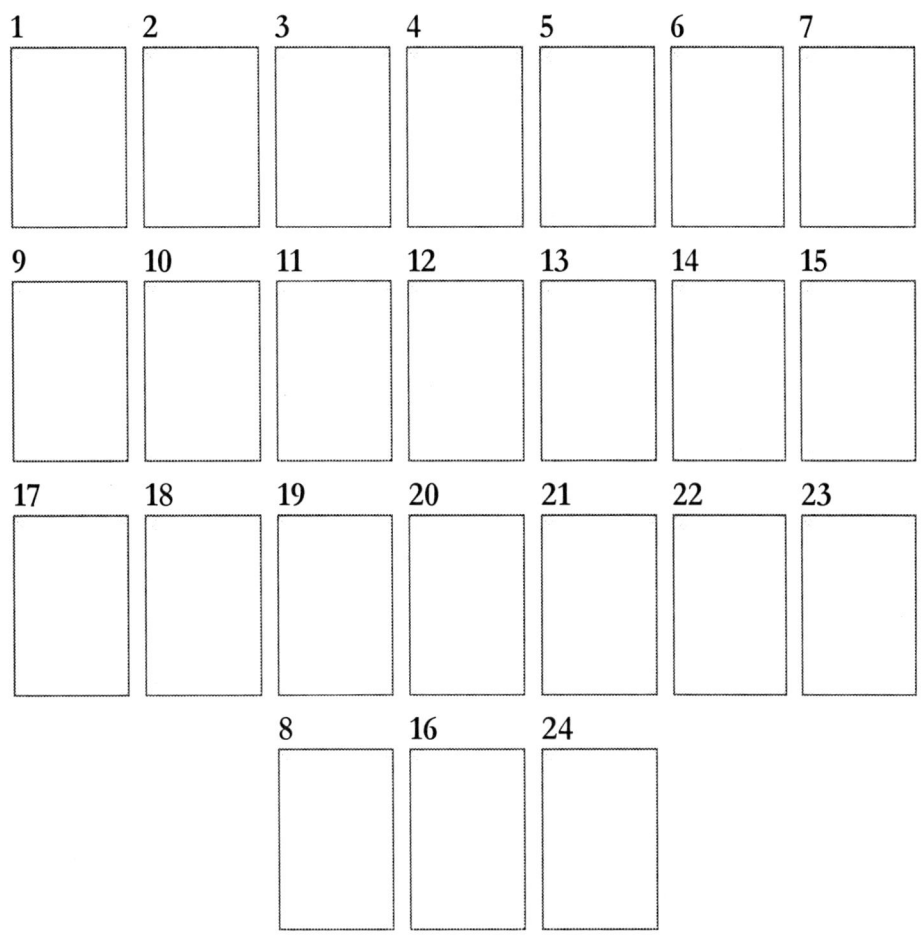

Name:................... Date:..................

Basic Interpretation:
....
....
....
....
....
....
....
....
....
....

The Moreau Spread

The Eight Card Spread

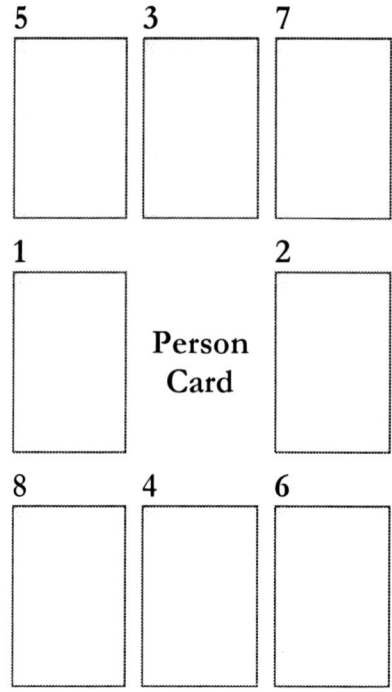

Name:……………… Date:……………..

Basic Interpretation:
………………………………………………………………………………………………
………………………………………………………………………………………………
………………………………………………………………………………………………
………………………………………………………………………………………………
………………………………………………………………………………………………
………………………………………………………………………………………………
………………………………………………………………………………………………
………………………………………………………………………………………………
………………………………………………………………………………………………
………………………………………………………………………………………………

The Eight Card Spread

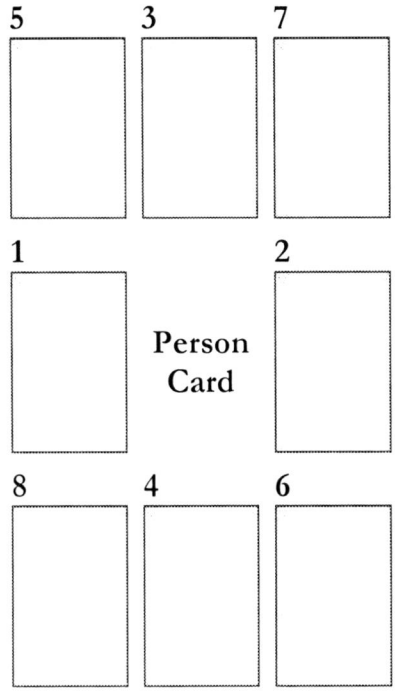

Name:.................... Date:..................

Basic Interpretation:
....
....
....
....
....
....
....
....
....
....

The Eight Card Spread

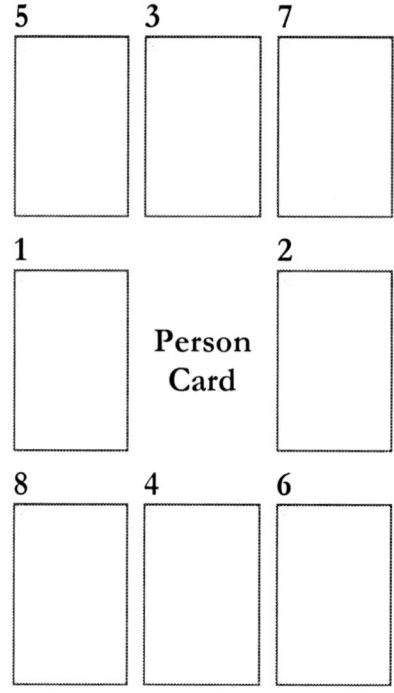

Name:................... Date:..................

Basic Interpretation:
....
....
....
....
....
....
....
....
....
....

The Eight Card Spread

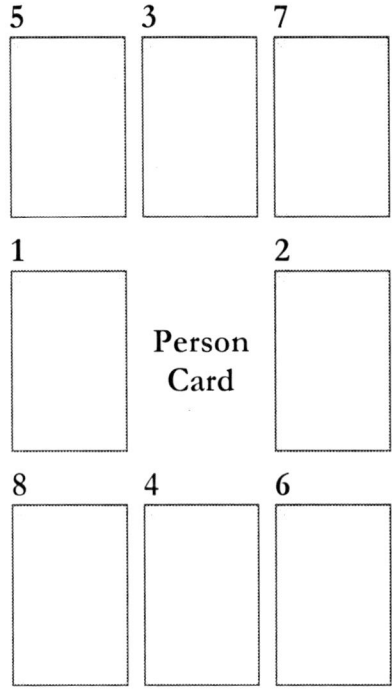

Name:................... Date:..................

Basic Interpretation:
....
....
....
....
....
....
....
....
....
....

APPENDIX
LENORMAND THROUGH THE YEARS

One of the main catch-phrases of our time is that 'the only Constant is Change' - this is definitely true for the Lenormand Fortune Telling Cards! Two years after Marie-Anne Lenormand's death, the publishing house Grimaud makes the first mention of a set of fortune telling cards called *Grand jeu de Mademoiselle Lenormand* - The Great Cards of Mlle Lenormand. This deck was created by a woman called Madame Breteau, who claimed to have been a student of Marie-Anne. Made up of 54 cards, the deck contained astrological symbols and depictions of Greek and Roman myths and legends. It is still available today. Not long after, several other European Publishing Houses and even Playing Card Manufacturers stared producing their own variations of the so called *Petit Lenormand* - the Small Lenormand deck. This appendix was added to show how the fortune telling cards of Mlle Lenormand have changed and developed over time. The last decade has seen a particular rise in interest in these cards and several smaller manufacturers and even individuals have published their own personal decks.

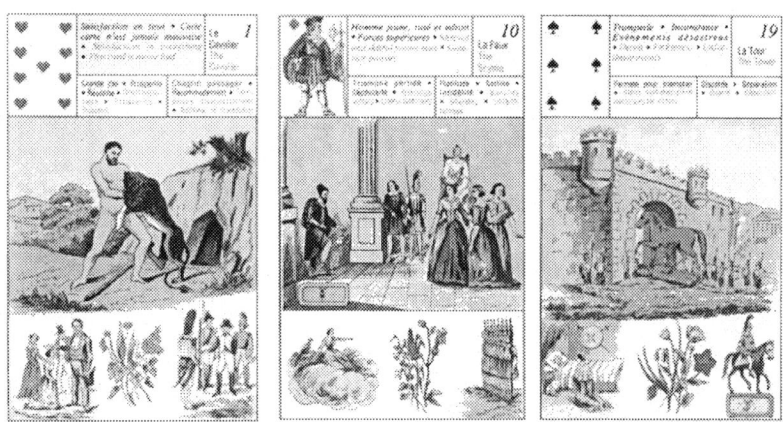

These are the original *Petit Lenormand* - still available from by Grimaud. These cards contain 'interpretation hints' in French and English. The set is sold as 36 cards + 1 additional card showing Mlle Lenormand.

Presented in a less elaborate fashion then *Petit Lenormand* this deck was published in the late 1800s and shows the symbolic meaning of the cards along with their corresponding playing cards.

These cards were published by the German publishing house G. Danner, Mühlhausen in 1890 and advertised as *'Madame Lenormands world-famous Fortune Telling Cards'*. They don't show the corresponding playing cards but have added 'magical symbols' to emphasise the mystical nature of fortune telling.

Less stylized but still fairly simple, these cards were published in 1890 by the German manufacterer Rühe.

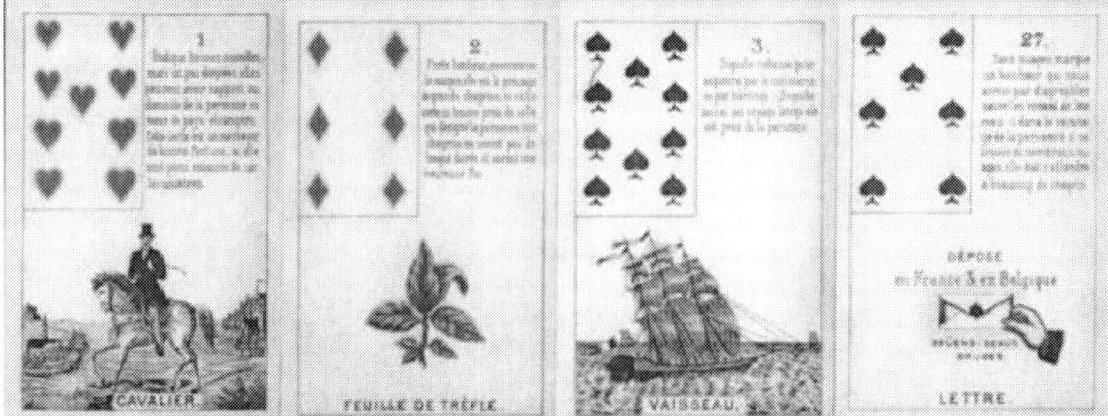

Sols as *Etit jeu Lenormand*, these cards already contain French phrases and poems related to their divinatory meaning. They were published by the Belgian publishing house Geuens-Seaux Bruges in 1890.

The US manufacturer Wehman Bros., New York published this deck in 1900. This deck was sold and advertised ad *Madame Le Normand's Gypsy Fortune Telling Card*.

Advertised as *Cartes Lenormand No. 1*, and published by the German manufacturer Dondorf around 1910, these cards resemble today's version of the Small Lenormand Deck most closely.

Advertised as *Cartes Lenormand No. 2*, and containing short poems related to their interpretation, these cards were also published by the German manufacturer Dondorf around 1910.

This modern version was published in 1950 by the German manufacturer VASS and advertised as *Lenormand Fortune Telling Cards with Pictures*. They are still available from the German manufacturer who is now known as ASS.

Known as *Jeu Lenormand - The Lenormand Cards*, and containing short poems related to their interpretation, this contemporary deck has first been published by Carta Mundi around 1980. Several other manufacturers have adopted the design and variations of these cards are now available in different languages.

This stunning deck, called Astrological Lenormand, was designed by Hildegard Leiding-Heinz and were published by the German manufacturer Verlag Weisse Reihe in 1998

Designed by Bruno Bieri and published as *Gypsy Lenormand Oracle Deck* by AG Müller Urania since 2005, these cards are meant to blend the symbolism of traditional Lenormand packs with the art of Gypsy fortune telling. The names of some of the cards of this deck were also changed. The Gentleman (Card 28) for example is here known as The Gypsy.

.

This deck is known as Lenormand Oracle Cards and has been published by Lo Scarabeo. The deck is sold with a 32 page booklet in English, Italian, Spanish, French and German.

This deck is known as Mystical Lenormand and was originally designed by Regula Elizabeth Fiechter and Urban Trösch. It is available since 2005 and has again changed some of the names of the cards. The Coffin (cards 8) shown as the 4th cards in the row above is here known as The Sarcophagus.

This deck is known as Flower Lenormand and was published by Carta Mundi. These cards are due to their popularity very hard to get.

BIBLIOGRAPHY

Bruno Bieri
> *'Zigeuner Lenormand Orakelkarten'*
> AGM, 1994

Catherine Yronwood
> *'Hoodoo Herb and Root Magic'*
> Lucky Mojo Curio Company, 2002

Christiane Renner
> *'Werken met de Waarzegkaarten van Mademoiselle Lenormand'*
> Uitgeverij, Amsterdam, 2001

Dietlind Herlert-Schaff
> *'Mystisches Kartenlegen nach Mlle Lenormand'*
> Corona, Hamburg, 1999

Fernandez Portugal Filhon
> *'Magias e Oferendas Afro-Brasileiras'*
> Madras, 2004

Maria Helena Farelli
> *'Pomba-Gira Cigana'*
> Pallas, Rio de Janeiro 2002

Mario dos Ventos
> - *'Na Gira do Exu - Invoking the Spirits of Brazilian Quimbanda'*
> Nzo Quimbanda Exu Ventania, London, 2006
> - *'The Black Book of Exu - Tapping into the power of the Master of Reality'*
> Nzo Quimbanda Exu Ventania, London, 2006
> - *'The Red Book of Pomba Gira - Tapping into the power of the Queen of the Night'*
> Nzo Quimbanda Exu Ventania, London, 2006
> - *'Sarava Umbanda - The Inner Workings of Macumba'*
> Nzo Quimbanda Exu Ventania, London, 2006

Nicholay de Matos
> *'Kiumbanda - A Grammar of the Art of Exu'*
> Chadezoad publishing, 2006

Zaydab Alkimin
> *'Zé Pelintra - Dono da Noite, Rei da Magia'*
> Pallas, Rio de Janeiro 2005

ABOUT THE AUTHOR

Mario dos Ventos lives in Surrey, United Kingdom. He is an initiated Quimbandeiro and spiritual head of *Nzo Quimbanda Exu Ventania*, a House of Quimbanda in the UK - a direct offspring of Nzila Aluvaia Kiumbanda Kimbiza, the Quimbanda House of Tata Remolino in Extrema, province of Minas Gerais, Brazil.

He is available for Lenormand Card Readings and consultations with the traditional Nzimbu/Nkobo Cowry Shell divination system - either in person (in the Greater London area) or over the internet and telephone (internationally) via: **http://www.erzulies.co.uk**

His homepage is **http://www.exu.moonfruit.com**

He can be contacted on: **casa_dos_ventos@hotmail.co.uk**

OTHER BOOKS BY THE SAME AUTHOR

NA GIRA DO EXU -
Invoking the Spirits of Brazilian Quimbanda

Quimbanda, the Cult of Exu and Pomba Gira, is a Shamanic Witchcraft Tradition practiced in Brazil. Sometimes called Macumba or even referred to as Satanism and Devil Worship, it incorporates elements of African and South-American Indian believes and religion as well as Medieval European Witchcraft.

Na Gira do Exu looks at the roots and historic development of Quimbanda, the role of the priesthood, ceremonies, magical workings and the hierarchy of the spirits of this cult. Over 300 Pontos (songs and invocations) and more then 100 Pontos Riscados (ritual sigils and drawings) for Exu are also included.

332 pages, 6.00' x 9.00'

Published by Nzo Quimbanda Exu Ventania - AVAILABLE AT **LULU.COM**

THE RED BOOK OF POMBA GIRA -
Tapping into the Power of the Queen of the Night

The Red Book of Pomba Gira celebrates the beauty, accessibility and value of Pomba Gira, the enchanted and seductive Queen of Brazilian Quimbanda. A practical guide for those interested in crude, old-fashioned European derived Witchcraft and Folk Magic, this book contains 25 magical workings, from economic improvement to spells for dealing with work and employment, romance and marriage. It shows how to approach Maria Mulambo for wealth and money, a working for love with Maria Padilha, how to defeat ones enemies with Rosa Caveira, a working to find true love with Pomba Gira Meninha, how to have success in business with Pomba Gira Cigana, what to for Pomba Gira da Luar to separate a couple and gives precise instructions on how to rid oneself of negative influences, stop gossip and slander and manifest health, wealth and happiness into ones life. Magical workings also include charms, amulets and talismans.

Rich in wisdom and advice, *The Red Book of Pomba Gira* inspires love and respect for Quimbanda, a tradition shrouded in mysteries and little known outside of Brazil.

148 pages, 6.00' x 9.00'

Published by Nzo Quimbanda Exu Ventania - AVAILABLE AT **LULU.COM**

THE BLACK BOOK OF EXU -

Tapping into the Power of the Master of Reality

The Black Book of Exu celebrates the power, accessibility and values of Exu, the powerful ruler of Quimbanda and Master of Reality. A practical guide for those interested in the practice of Afro-Brazilian Witchcraft, this book contains 27 magical workings, from economic improvement to spells for dealing with work and employment and how to defeat one's enemies.

It shows how to approach Exu Chama Dinheiro to gain wealth, how to solve any problem with the law by the aid of Exu Sete Encruzilhadas, how to get rid of ones enemies with the help of Exu das Matas, how to safe someone from death invoking the help of Exu Omulu, how to protect a house or temple with the aid of Exu Porteira, and gives precise instructions on how to rid oneself of negative influences, stop gossip and slander and manifest health, wealth and happiness into ones life. Workings also include powders, amulets and talismans.

Rich in wisdom and advice, *The Black Book of Exu* inspires love and respect for Quimbanda, a tradition shrouded in mysteries and little known outside of Brazil.

158 pages, 6.00' x 9.00'

Published by Nzo Quimbanda Exu Ventania - AVAILABLE AT **LULU.COM**

SARAVA UMBANDA!
The Inner Workings of Macumba

Drawing on the teachings and practices of different Umbanda Temples in Brazil, this landmark book, which contains 45 chapters, spread over more then 380 pages, explain the history, cosmology and theology of Umbanda, look at ceremonies, the organizational structure of individual centers and the pantheon of this religion. This book also explains Umbanda Initiation, the 'necklaces of the worshipers', gives recipes for orixa food offerings and special workings for cleansings, prosperity, luck, love and happiness.

Also included is an appendix containing a collection of Pontos Cantados (sung invocations) for all the lines of spirits and orixas of Umbanda. A special part of this book is also dedicated to the application of Umbanda outside of Brazil. What problems and pitfalls can be encountered when practicing this religion, which is tied to the land, outside of its country of origin? What new challenges must be faced and how can we adapt without compromising the roots, values and believes of Umbanda?

384 pages, 8.50' x 11.00'

Published by Nzo Quimbanda Exu Ventania - AVAILABLE AT **LULU.COM**

SEA EL SANTISIMO
Working the Spirits in Espiritismo and Espiritismo Cruzado

Whilst there are many different types of spiritual religions throughout the world, Caribbean Spiritism is a very unique spiritist traditon of Cuba and Puerto Rico. Known as Espiritismo or Espiritismo Cruzado, it is often compared to Brazilian Umbanda due to its 'crossing' with Palo Monte Mayombe and Santeria (African Congo and Yoruba practices).

Jam-packed with invocations and prayers, 'Sea el Santisimo' contains detailed information and instructions on how to set up and work a Boveda and how to do novenas and special workings for the saints and spirits of the dead.

All prayers for Mesa Espiritual that have previously been published in Allan Kardec's "Collection of Selected Prayers" are given in a new, fresh and devotional translation. Songs for Mesa Espiritual and prayers for spirits such as La Madama, El Congo and many of the saints make this book an alternative primer for the practice of Espiritismo and 'Espiritismo Cruzado'.

256 pages, 6.00" x 9.00"

Published by Nzo Quimbanda Exu Ventania - AVAILABLE AT LULU.COM

FURTHER STUDY

The Lenormand Fortune-Telling Course

Designed for those who seek to delve deeper into the mysterious world of the Fortune Telling Cards of Mlle Lenormand, *The Lenormand Fortune-Telling Course* offers a year-long training program in this exceptional divination system.

The course shows how to use the cards to execute special readings for love and relationships, finances as well as work and employment. Extended information on each individual card, several different spreads and instruction on how to use these cards even for dream interpretation are also integrated in this thorough program. Additional hints and tips for aspiring professional readers show how to use these cards to their full potential!

This course is send by post and includes 1 set of the *1941 Mlle Lenormand Cartomancy Deck*, 12 lessons and 4 assignments which should be retuned by email. A printed Certificate of Completion will also be issued after the program.

Please visit **http://www.botanica.moonfruit.com/course**
or email **casa_dos_ventos@hotmail.co.uk**
to join this course

Printed in the United States
111567LV00003B/52/A